Your Playbook For Tough Times:
Living Large On Small Change,
For The Short Term Or The Long Haul

By Donna Freedman

Word Matters Press

Copyright 2016

ISBN 978-0-9978216-0-4

ISBN 978-0-9978216-1-1 (ebook)

Note: This book contains several affiliate links.

What the experts say about Your Playbook For Tough Times:

"Donna writes with a laser-sharp focus on strategies that will help you through tough times. Unlike most personal finance books, her money-saving tips aren't meant to be cute; they're real strategies based on tough times she's successfully overcome in her own life. Donna's advice can inspire hope if you feel that you've reached a personal or financial dead end."

– **Clark Howard,** consumer expert and nationally syndicated radio host

"Frugality is not a dirty word – it's a lifesaver. And who better to teach you than Donna Freedman? She's been where you are now, she understands what you're going through and best of all, she knows the way out. Deciding to read this book could be that one decision that stands between you and a totally different life."

– **Mary Hunt**, creator of Debt-Proof Living and author of more than three dozen personal finance books

"A clear, concise and complete guide that will help you change your life. As someone with more than 30 years in the financial planning and personal finance writing fields, I can attest that you won't find a better step-by-step guide anywhere."

– **Gary Foreman**, The Dollar Stretcher

"This is an essential manual for anyone aiming to live large on a small budget. Going through tough times? This book's for you. Worried about tough times looming on the horizon? This book's for you, too. This book is even for you if things *aren't* tough but you're curious about sensible ways to make your money last longer. One of a small number of books that has earned a permanent place on my reference shelf."

– **J.D. Roth**, founder of Get Rich Slowly and Money Boss and author of *Your Money: The Missing Manual*

"Unlike a lot of people writing about personal finance, Donna Freedman knows first-hand what it's like to be broke. She knows how to survive tough times, to live well on less and to create a good life even when bad things happen. Donna imparts all this wisdom with empathy and compassion – along with the occasional kick in the butt. She's also one of the funniest people you'll ever have the pleasure of reading, so get started already!"

– **Liz Weston**, author of *The 10 Commandments Of Money, Deal With Your Debt, Easy Money* and *Your Credit Score: How to Improve the 3-Digit Number That Shapes Your Financial Future*

"Too often the standard financial advice doesn't account for devastating circumstances. Donna knows life doesn't always go as planned, and her book offers practical financial strategies for anyone who (wants) real-world advice for moving forward."

– **Miranda Marquit**, Planting Money Seeds and Adulting.tv

"The great thing about *Your Playbook For Tough Times* is that it's not just advice to use when the going gets tough. It's advice that, when followed, will keep you from experiencing tough times in the first place. This should be required reading for everyone, whether starting out or starting over."

– **Stacy Johnson**, founder of Money Talks News

"No one anticipates it, but for the many people without sufficient emergency savings – and that may be almost everyone – economic disaster could be just a divorce, a stretch of unemployment or an illness away. Not only can (this book) help you negotiate the Byzantine world of social services, it can provide self-help ideas that you may never have thought of...Sympathetic and supportive, Donna's book can effectively hold your hand as you inch your way back to solvency."

– **Kathy Kristof,** contributing editor at Kiplinger's Personal Finance, CBS MoneyWatch columnist and editor of KathyKristof.com

"The ultimate guide to cutting costs, getting spending under control and taking charge of your finances. Whether you're struggling to pull yourself out of a bad financial situation or just want to start living a more frugal life so you have more money to enjoy the things that really matter to you, you'll find the advice you need in this book."

– **Cameron Huddleston**, award-winning personal finance journalist

"Donna mixes straight talk with a deep sense of compassion; she understands the reasons people can wind up in money trouble but expects them to use her tips to take charge of their lives. With her distinctive voice and trademark humor, the author gives readers the tools they need to create that change."

– **Stephanie Nelson**, CouponMom.com

Dedicated to some of the people (can't possibly list them *all*) who have made a huge difference in my life personally and/or professionally: Linda Billingsley, Linda Billington, Will Chen, MP Dunleavey, Glendon and Priscilla Fisher, GW Fisher, Geneva Hanes, Stacy Johnson, Harlan Landes, Rebecca and Doug Lyon, Joshua McCoy, J. Money, Abigail and Tim Perry, J.D. Roth and Phil Taylor.

Thanks to Meghan Pembleton for expert proofreading and editing. (You should hire her.)

A special shout-out to Des Toups and Liz Weston: If not for them, I wouldn't be a personal finance writer.

Enormous and eternal appreciation to DF, my frugal partner. Couldn't make it without him.

Table Of Contents

Introduction

For the past decade I've been writing about personal finance and frugality for some of the top personal finance sites on the Web. But that's not the only reason you should listen to me. Here's the real scoop: *I've lived this stuff.* The information in my book has been personally field-tested – three times! (More on that in a minute.)

I'm not an elitist who's never had to worry about money. I know what it's like to live in the cheap (read: dangerous) part of a big city, to stand in line at a social services agency, to empty a piggy bank for bus fare on payday. So trust me when I say this book will help three different groups of people:

- **Those already in tough times** due to un- or underemployment, illness or a heavy debt load.

- **Those anticipating tough times,** such as a new or worsening medical condition or the layoffs sweeping through your workplace.

- **Those who want to live lean to realize a dream**, such as early retirement, full-time parenthood or entrepreneurship.

My mantra has long been "Save where you can so you can spend where you want" – in other words, living intentionally. I encourage readers to make choices with care and purpose, rather than letting life just happen to them.

During my three decades as a journalist I've talked with a lot of people who saw money as a chaotic, uncontrollable force. I heard them express worldviews along the lines of:

You either have money or you don't.

People like us will always be in some kind of debt.

If you do get some money/some credit, live a little! You could die tomorrow.

It's true that some of us have less – maybe a lot less – than others. **But we can choose how to use the money we get**. The financial bottom line isn't just about what you earn, but also about how much of it you can keep.

Never giving up

I learned this during my own (three!) encounters with tough times:

- As a 16-year-old charged with running a household of three people after my parents split up. Every two weeks my dad gave me $100 for groceries and supplies. I took great pride in giving $40 or even $60 back to him.

- As a broke 21-year-old single mom in Philadelphia, so strapped for funds that I ate dry-bean soup almost every day and did all our laundry (including diapers) on a scrub-board in the kitchen sink.

- As a woman in her late 40s, broke once again from a protracted divorce and supporting a disabled adult child – all while *finally* getting a college degree.

Each of those times it would have been so easy to give up. How many teens would simply have refused to take on all the housework? Let alone cook and bake everything from scratch, preserve garden produce and hang out laundry before catching the school bus at 6:45 a.m.? I probably should have asked for help, but I made it through with determination and Clorox. (Also, sadly, with an ulcer.)

Four years later some people shook their heads over my decision to keep the baby: I had no husband, no education, no full-time job, no car, no prospects. Yet I've never regretted the decision to raise my daughter. In fact, it's the best thing I've ever done – and despite my lack of a diploma I eventually clawed my way into a job as a newspaper reporter, winning regional and national awards.

When I finally got the courage to leave an abusive marriage my finances went so far south they were practically north once more. I juggled freelance writing, an apartment-building management gig and whatever odd jobs I could find while undergoing much-needed therapy. During that time I cut my spending to the bone to pay for my daughter's needs and throw every possible dollar at my divorce attorney bill (which was like trying to melt a glacier with an Aim 'n' Flame.)

Yet I knew that things would get better one day. To paraphrase a popular T-shirt slogan, tough times don't last – because tough people can outlast them.

And that's what happened. Within a couple of years I'd earned a full scholarship to the University of Washington while still working a crazy-quilt of part-time jobs. That's when I wrote a guest post for MSN Money, "Surviving (And Thriving) on $12,000 A Year." Delighted by the enormous reader reaction, the editor commissioned additional pieces on frugal living. These articles appealed to an audience that hadn't been reached before, i.e., people who *weren't* well-off.

About eight months later I was tasked with creating MSN's Smart Spending blog. Not long after that the great recession hit in earnest – and suddenly everybody needed advice. How to cut costs. How to juggle card balances. How to pack a lunch, for heaven's sake. Personal finance blogs flourished because people who'd always done just fine were now up to their hairlines in debt – and utterly terrified.

Smart Spending and other PF sites introduced them to concepts like budgeting, nixing impulse purchases, building an emergency fund, using coupons, living with roommates and driving a car until the wheels fell off. Readers started bragging in the comments section about hypermiling and dumpster diving, or the fact that they'd learned to cook and entertain at home. Frugal wardrobes! Frugal holidays! Frugal travel!

Apparently those lessons didn't stick. Bling is now back and frugality is *so* 2008. As Mark Twain once wrote, history doesn't repeat itself but it does rhyme.

Staying in the game

Not everyone has recovered from the recession, however. Some folks still struggle to stay afloat – getting ahead is a distant dream – and others are wondering just where their money goes.

If either of those situations sounds familiar, you'll be (grimly) pleased to know that it isn't just you. Even fairly well-off U.S. residents find themselves living paycheck to paycheck – and often it has nothing to do with overspending on frills. In the past 20 years our median net worth has decreased by about 21 percent overall. However, for the working class – those who earn between $23,300 and $40,499 – median net worth dropped more than 50 percent.

That's why I wrote this book. I want to provide information that helps people live their best lives – and to do this with the money they have.

Your Playbook For Tough Times is a primer on making careful and creative decisions about money. These choices will keep you in the game during a crisis, help you pare expenses during a slowdown or let you to squirrel away dollars to reach a personal goal.

What you won't find in this book? Victim-blaming. The financial advice from ivory towers (and sometimes even from popular bloggers) too often has the same underpinnings:

If you're in money trouble it's probably your own damn fault.

You must be shiftless and/or stupid.

But you can fix things by cutting back on lattes/selling toys/getting a side hustle/using the envelope system.

Those last few suggestions aren't bad advice as such. Yet core issues like being born into poverty and/or an economically depressed region, stagnant salaries, lack of education (or its opposite, high student loan repayments), tax increases and health problems can't be solved with a handful of coupons and a brown-bag lunch.

And even if you *did* make some poor financial choices, what difference does that make now? Self-recrimination won't get you anywhere. It just plants you more firmly where you are, i.e., mired in fear and self-loathing.

Or maybe you were left holding the bag due to divorce, job loss or serious illness. Believe me: I know just how much that stinks. But unless your fairy godmother drops off a winning Powerball ticket, you have to play the hand you were dealt.

Deciding to change

During my own difficult times I'd sometimes wonder, "Why me?" Ultimately I realized the answer was, "Why *not* me?" Stuff happens. *Life* happens. It's not personal. Maybe it's unfair, but it's not personal. So I worked to fix what I could and made my peace with the rest of it.

Use the material in this book to take charge of what *you* can fix, or at least affect. For example, you can't change the fact that your spouse is on disability. However, you *can* reduce the impact by learning to budget, locating relevant social services, and focusing not just on getting through each day but also on being happy with the here and now. (Hint: A rich life is not necessarily determined by the number of dollar signs in it.)

At times this could feel difficult or even impossible. **But if you do nothing, then nothing will change.** Your debt won't go away. Your job situation won't improve. Your kids will need more, not less, as they grow. Your retirement will get closer every day, whether or not you've done a thing to prepare for it.

Acknowledge the dark clouds, then visualize their silver linings: *If I am willing to work at it, I can almost certainly change my life.*

Although it's up to you to do the work, I'm here to help. Think of the book as me whispering money-saving tips into your ear, or holding your hand as you put names to your goals and then bring those dreams to fruition.

Dare to change your life. Start today.

1: The Financial Fire Drill

Food, shelter, clothing and utilities are needs. The rest is just a series of wants.

Sound stark? It is. There's not a whole lot of margin when times are tight or when you've got a bold dream like retiring early or starting your own business.

But the needs/wants binary isn't a form of punishment. It's the basis of intentional living, i.e., choosing where your money will (and won't) be going.

It's also an integral part of what I call the "financial fire drill," a kind of extreme budget makeover. The idea isn't that you won't pay your bills, but rather that you'll find ways to cut the number of bills you have to pay.

The financial fire drill is about smart use of available funds. It's also pretty simple:

- On paper, build a baseline budget – the absolute minimum you need to survive.
- Pretend that your household lost some or all of its income.
- Subtract the baseline from the income that remains (including unemployment, if that's an option). If the answer is a negative number, time to take another look at those wants and needs.

Obviously if you've already lost a lot (or all) of your income then you need a baseline budget more than ever. This should include basic shelter, food, clothing, utilities, debt service and entertainment.

Note: "Basic" means exactly that. Figure out on paper how little you could get away with spending – without jeopardizing health or safety or turning into a deadbeat.

For example, you'd nix meals out in favor of food cooked at home, but would make sure those meals were nutritious and tasty as well as cheap. Living solely on ramen and oatmeal wouldn't do you much good.

You'd cut the cable in favor of Hulu and/or Netflix, or at least drop down to a basic package. Although cutting television entirely has its charms – I haven't had a TV since 2005 – going cold turkey is not for everyone (especially shut-ins).

While you'd keep making essential payments (e.g., child support) in full, you would stop paying extra on a mortgage, student loan or consumer debt. Hobbies, nights out and the kids' extracurricular activities would be cut to a minimum; some of these things could be halted altogether, at least for a while.

Finally, you should make it your business to know the price of nearby rentals and the cost of moving, should that become necessary. (It probably won't.)

Additional steps to take

You've got a baseline budget. Great! But that's just the start.

Got education debt? Investigate loan deferment and forbearance (https://studentaid.ed.gov/sa/repay-loans/deferment-forbearance) *before* you need to consider them. If you've got consumer debt, now is the time to cut back on nonessential spending and focus on paying off those credit cards.

Have a heart-to-heart with your insurance agent. Ask how much you would save by raising your deductibles or whether it's appropriate to drop collision. If you plan to stop driving for a while, get quotes for the most basic policy. Don't cancel your insurance entirely, since it can be tough and/or pricier to get a new policy after a period of non-coverage.

Call utility providers to find out if any offer reduced rates for folks in financial trouble. (Learn more about this in Chapter 8.)

Make a list of what you could sell, should it come to that. Electronics, bicycles, collectibles, even your childhood toys might fetch a fair amount. Hey, someone paid me $1,200 for a little plastic baseball figurine. Do a little research and find out what those American Girl dolls are worth.

In anticipation of layoffs, work on your résumé and investigate job re-training opportunities in your area. Nose around for additional money-making options: contracting gigs, a part-time job, a side hustle. (Chapter 9 holds opportunities you might never have imagined.)

Now: Put everything you've learned in a file folder marked "Financial Fire Drill," and put it someplace handy. With luck you'll never need to use it.

The good news

Initially the idea might be about as pleasant as thinking about a colonoscopy. You know you *should* do it, but you're a little afraid of what you might find out. (*What if I can't make it on unemployment?* or *What if our household can't make it on one salary?*)

However, a financial fire drill can actually be reassuring: *If push came to shove, we could manage on as little as $1,000 a month.* Cutting expenses, even on paper, can be liberating.

The good news: You might learn that simply trimming the budgetary fat would be more than enough to offset any lost income. (Frugal tip: Start cutting back a little right now, then bank those savings in an emergency fund. Or put them toward retirement.)

The better news: You could add expenses back in as your financial situation improves.

The best news: When that time came you might find you were doing just fine with less. I'm no minimalist, but let me say this: Having fewer needs means more room in your life as well as in your budget.

Like all fire drills, this is an "in case of emergency" safety move. Relatively few schools (or homes) burn down. But it's still a good idea to know what to do if that happens.

2: Your Frugal Arsenal

This chapter is full of what I like to think of as "weapons against waste." These hacks will help you turn your money woes around. That's because you'll be:

- Finding the lowest prices every time you shop (only amateurs pay retail)
- Adding extra layers of savings with relative ease
- Using coupons without pain – no more clipping unless you really want to
- Getting items for free (including cash in the form of PayPal)

These simple yet magic formulas apply to multiple aspects of your budget, including education, entertainment, pets, shopping, special occasions and even health care.

Keep in mind that not every tactic works for every person. Pick the ones that are easiest and/or get you the best results. Don't try too many at once, lest you become overwhelmed.

Once you arm yourself with these weapons, you'll wonder why you ever paid full price.

1. Getting paid to shop

Attention, Internet shoppers: You can get money back on almost anything you want to buy online. Cash-back shopping sites such as Mr. Rebates, DollarDig, Extrabux, FatWallet, Ebates, ShopAtHome and Big Crumbs offer rebates of up to 20 percent on a huge variety of goods and services.

These cash-back sites get affiliate fees when they send buyers to online retailers. Then they share a slice of that fee with us, the shoppers. Simply begin your trip at the cash-back site vs. going directly to your favorite store's website. Fail to do so and your potential savings become money left on the table, when all it would have taken is that one extra click.

Note: This isn't just for holiday and birthday buying. Savvy shoppers can use cash-back sites to take care of daily needs, including but certainly not limited to diapers, contact lenses, vitamins, pet supplies, furniture, home-improvement items, office supplies, paper goods and drugstore items. You can also get money back for subscribing to magazines, renting a car, using tax-prep software, filtering your water, booking airline travel, registering a domain name, doing genealogical research or even joining a dating service.

It's pretty easy to do:

- Start every shopping trip at one of those cash-back sites.
- Click on the store where you want to shop.
- Buy what you want.
- Wait for the money to be credited to your account.

A few caveats apply. (Don't they always?) To make the most of your experience, see the "Ultimate Guide to Cash Back Shopping" on the Wise Bread blog (http://www.wisebread.com/ultimate-guide-to-cash-back-shopping).

2. Your retail concierge

If you want the best deals, get yourself a (virtual) personal shopper. Price comparison sites like PriceGrabber.com, NexTag and FatWallet exist to tell you how to pay the smallest amount for the items you need.

Some offer additional services, such as price alerts, and all offer online discount codes. At least one such aggregator (FatWallet) is also a cash-back shopping site.

These sites are particularly great at finding hot deals from lesser-known merchants that you might never find on your own. Some niche companies operate *only* online and have better prices than the big-name retailers.

However, shopping this way is like pricing airline tickets – those screamin' deals may not last. Prices can change quickly, possibly even in a few minutes because closeout items can sell quickly and promotions may be short-lived. Make sure you're looking at the true final cost, too; if sales tax and shipping get applied, a deal could morph from awesome to average.

And remember: *A low price is not an excuse to spend.* If you can't afford it and/or don't really need it, there's no such thing as a deal that's too good to pass up.

3. Not your grandmother's coupons

Old-school coupon clipping/filing/matching wasn't for everyone. But times have changed and you'll find more virtual than paper Qs these days. Download them to your store loyalty card(s) and you're done

In addition, you can rely on coupon/deal bloggers to do the matchups for you. For example, each week sites like CouponMom.com and A Full Cup do a state-by-state, store-by-store linking of Qs and sales at supermarkets, discount emporia like Target and Wal-Mart, drugstores and even dollar stores.

Look for regional deal bloggers, too, as they may provide up-to-the-minute tips on sales they encounter personally. ("The Walgreens on Minnesota Drive has a huge table of diapers for a buck a bag! Get over there!")

Despite these consumer-friendly developments, coupon myths still abound. Among the most common misunderstandings:

Myth: They're just for junk food.

Reality: Sure, you'll see plenty of discounts for empty calories and colors not found in nature. You'll also find Qs for non-sugary cereal (including oatmeal), canned beans, canned and frozen vegetables, fresh produce and even organic items. Pick your spots! Blogger and author Lauren Greutman feeds her family a gluten-free, organic diet and she's one heck of a coupon hacker.

Myth: The savings aren't worth your time.

Reality: That depends on what you think your time is worth. Do you get paid for every single moment you're awake? I don't. Getting free or nearly free toiletries and food products helped me a lot when I was broke and even allowed me to donate some items to a shelter and a food bank. Maybe that's you, too. (Frugal tip: Some of those freebies also work well as stocking stuffers.)

Myth: Coupons encourage overbuying.

Reality: Stephanie Nelson of CouponMom.com talks about "strategic shopping," the combining of coupons and great sales to save up to 50 percent on your monthly food bill. If diced tomatoes are a quarter a can and your family eats a lot of homemade chili, why *not* overbuy? Otherwise you'll have to pay full price for tomatoes later on. Use as many coupons as you can to stock up on items that will let you save money on future food bills.

Maximize your savings

Look for coupons online (the coupon/deal sites often link to downloadable Qs) and/or use the Favado coupon app (http://www.savings.com/favado/).

You can get extra paper coupons by:

- Asking family/friends to save you the Sunday inserts

- Stopping in at coffeehouses and fast food restaurants, where Sunday newspapers are often read and tossed aside
- Checking the recycle bins in your apartment building or workplace
- Starting a "coupon cooperative" – a small group of like-minded shoppers who meet every so often to trade Qs

Note: It is against the law to buy or sell coupons. Don't do it.

A few more tactics

Coupons exist for non-grocery items, too. Websites like Savings.com, FatWallet and Retail Me Not provide discount codes and may have their own proprietary coupons. Before you buy *anything*, from asparagus to zoot suits, visit these sites and type in the name of the store(s) where you want to shop.

Follow your favorite retailers on Facebook and/or Twitter. You might get exclusive codes that way.

Buying online and not in a rush? Leave the website with the item still in your shopping cart. Within a couple of days the retailer will likely e-mail you a discount code to entice you into completing the purchase.

Be sure to check the total amount before you hit "purchase." If the discount wasn't applied it may have expired, in which case you need to look for another one. It's also possible that you spelled it wrong.

Finally, check local shopper publications (in my area it's called "Good Deals" magazine) and those blue ValPak envelopes. Use a buy-one-get-one coupon the next time it's your turn to buy lunch. Grab that portrait package special for your son's senior photos. Or maybe you never thought of using coupons for oil changes, dental visits or windshield replacement. *Start* thinking about it.

So you've found the best possible price, the retailer has a store near you or you can access it through a cash-back shopping site, and you've got a free shipping code and a 20-percent-off coupon. You can actually improve the deal further by paying part or all of the tab with….

4. Discounted gift cards: Another layer of savings

Gift cards bought on the secondary market can save you big bucks on everyday purchases and on special occasions. Sites like Cardpool, Raise and ABC Gift Cards place unwanted scrip into good homes.

Why are they unwanted? Several possible reasons:

- The card is inconvenient to use (the nearest Regal Cinema is two bus rides away)
- The card wasn't a good fit (think, "Texas Roadhouse card given to a vegetarian")
- The recipient would frankly rather have the money

Cards for popular stores like Wal-Mart and Target usually come in at about 3 percent off, but the majority are discounted from 10 to 25 percent. Use the plastic to pay for all sorts of things: groceries, gasoline, pet supplies, drugstore purchases, haircuts, shoes, movie tickets, even trips to the dollar store.

Since different resellers offer different percentages, search for the best price on the aggregator site Gift Card Granny. You can also set up an alert for a card you want but don't see listed.

A few tips:

- See if the best deal is from a reseller you can access through a cash-back shopping site. You'll get a rebate of up to 1.5 percent on your purchase – not enough to retire on, but still another layer of savings.

- Guard your cards. They're as good as cash so if you lose them, you lose out. A free app called Gyft will store card info so you can leave the plastic at home.

- Got unwanted cards of your own? The reseller sites will buy them from you. Thus that $25 Applebee's card your boss gave you for Christmas – which isn't enough to cover dinner for both you and your spouse – will do you some good after all.

- Think ahead. Your kids are going to keep outgrowing their shoes and your dog is always going to be hungry, so send away for Payless ShoeSource or PetSmart scrip *before* it's needed. A couple of years ago I saved a little over $107 on a home-improvement project by ordering discounted Home Depot gift cards through a cash-back shopping site.

Believe it or not, there's still another way to get a better deal, if you…

5. Pay with *free* gift cards

Most of us have been spammed with e-mails or startled by pop-ups along the lines of, *"CONGRATULATIONS! YOU JUST WON A $100 GIFT CARD!"*

Don't believe it. To get the "free" prize you'd have to buy something (or maybe more than one something) and jump through virtual hoops (maybe several of them) – and if you did that, you'd probably be tormented by future spam and telemarketing efforts.

However, it actually is possible to get gift cards for free. Kind of. Hardly anything in life is truly free.

You'll have to work with a specific search engine, click on e-mails, use a certain type of credit card or purchase a few things you were going to buy anyway. Mostly, all it will cost you is time – a few minutes a day or more, if you've got them.

How much time do you spend in a day staring into the fridge wondering what to fix for lunch, or into the closet as you decide what to wear? Do you watch a lot of TV or play games? Free up some of those minutes to take advantage of card-earning opps.

The granddaddy of them all

Probably the oldest of the rewards sites is MyPoints, which has been around since 2000. Members earn points for reading e-mails, watching short videos, taking surveys or buying things through MyPoints links.

Assuming that you clicked on just three e-mails a day, you'd earn 5,475 points per year. That alone would be enough to pay for a $25 gift card and, depending on the category, almost enough for $50 worth of scrip. Add some surveys, videos or shopping and your totals rise even faster.

Cash in for gift cards that pay for necessities (clothing, shoe, drug and department stores) or treats (movies, restaurants, sports gear). Or, maybe, for special occasions: My daughter, her fiancé and I saved MyPoints for about a year and a half, then traded them in for Wal-Mart cards. We used them at Sam's Club to pay for most of the food for their wedding reception.

Some pretty nice Swag

My favorite rewards program, hands-down, is Swagbucks, a site that gives points for Internet searches, watching videos, playing online games, taking surveys and shopping through the site portal. (If you're not a member, please consider joining with my referral code: http://www.swagbucks.com/refer/Newlife1114.)

The site randomly awards online searches with points called SBs – anywhere from four to 100 at a time. During the day one or more "Swag Codes" will be released, good for extra points; periodically the company stages "Swag Code Extravaganzas," with at least six codes in a day.

Swagbucks also has team challenges, which give users a chance to earn extra points. One of the easiest ways to earn, however, is to refer others, because you get 10 percent of any points they earn, forever.

The downside: All the gift cards are e-codes vs. physical ones, although these days most people are fine with getting and using codes. My favorite e-code is for Amazon.

The major upside: **Swagbucks offers a PayPal option**. In other words, you can trade in your points for cash as long as you have a PayPal account – and who couldn't use a little more folding green?

Bottoms up!

I drink a can of Diet Coke every day or two, which isn't the best thing in the world for me. But what's life without a *little* sin? Especially if I can profit (albeit slowly) from the vice?

My Coke Rewards is a rewards program that's really helped my holidays. You enter points found inside bottle caps and multipacks, then cash in for premiums that include e-gift cards. Brands include Amazon, Barnes & Noble, Sephora, iTunes, Nike, Target, Petco, Gamestop, Gap Inc., Bass Pro Shops and TJ Maxx/Marshalls/HomeGoods.

Here's the beauty part: You don't actually have to drink Coke products (including Minute Maid juices and Dasani flavored waters) to participate. I've interviewed people who get them from friends and family members, or who harvest these things by the hundreds at workplaces, community festivals and recycling centers.

Incidentally, you can also trade in points for…coupons for free 12-packs of Coke products. *#greatcycleoflife*

Save as many as you can by December, though, because that's when My Coke Rewards puts some of its most popular premiums on sale – including things like Amazon gift cards and AMC movie tickets. One year I was able to get those 12-pack coupons for just 30 points.

Additional options

Bloggers who want to call attention to their sites offer periodic giveaways. I do this myself almost weekly and I can say that nothing pulls in pageviews like the chance to win a gift card. (Especially if it's for Amazon, Starbucks or any movie theater.)

Hitting Google with "gift card giveaways [current year]" will result in many options but again, be careful: Some of these places might be marketers trolling for info. My advice is to start a separate e-mail address just for such contests, because you will be spammed. Personally, I'd never enter a contest that needs my phone number, and I also tend to use my P.O. box vs. my home address.

Keep an eye out for "free gift card" promos in stores. Target does this a lot, e.g., "Buy $30 worth of [whatever] and receive a $10 Target card." Genius, really, since it's something that you can spend *only* by returning to Target. Again, if you were planning to buy [whatever] anyway, then why not get a $10 head start on your next [whatever]? I've seen the same maneuver in supermarkets (rarely the ones where I live, unfortunately, but I can always hope).

6. Reward yourself

Finally, there's the option of rewards credit cards. You might not be eligible if you have a low credit score or don't earn much money right now. However, if you already have a credit card you might be able to parlay it into another brand with a rewards program.

I have three such cards and use the points to pay for holiday and special-occasion shopping. They also come in handy when I visit my daughter and son-in-law, because cashing in for restaurant gift cards lets me take them out to eat without breaking my budget.

Compare rewards-card deals at these links:

- http://www.beverlyharzog.com/category/credit-card-reviews/
- http://www.cardratings.com/rewardpoints.html?src=61 0567
- https://www.nerdwallet.com/the-best-credit-cards#rewards

Note: Some frugality experts think that credit is a terrible idea. "Cash is king!" they trumpet, pretending that the current credit-score system doesn't exist. Ignore credit cards and/or personal loans entirely at your own peril, however. If you don't have a credit history you'll pay more – probably a *lot* more – for things like vehicle loans, insurance and mortgages.

Is that fair? Not particularly. But it's the system we have right now. A savvy consumer will learn to work within it.

Myself, I'm a firm believer in having at least two credit cards in case of serious emergencies. On a couple of occasions I've had to fly out of town on a few hours' notice when family members became critically ill.

If you know from painful experience that you can't be trusted around plastic, don't get one. But workarounds probably exist, such as stashing the card with a trusted family member or friend, or storing the card in that person's safe-deposit box. Decide ahead of time what constitutes an "emergency," though. (Putting it in writing might help.)

Once I interviewed a woman whose solution to impulse spending was to tape the card against the back of an extremely heavy armoire. She then had her boyfriend push it against a wall. The woman couldn't so much as budge the piece on her own, but if a true emergency were to arise he would come over to retrieve the card for her. (Hey, whatever works.)

Amassing points in this manner may sound slow, and it generally is. But frugality sometimes works this way, i.e., small steps that lead to bigger rewards.

3: Savvy Consumer Hacks – Simple Tactics That Save You Thousands

The tools from Chapter 2 will quickly become second nature. So, too, will the following smart consumer behaviors.

Not all of these tactics apply universally. For example, if you don't do any online shopping you won't care about the amazin' Amazon hacks. But several of these techniques will work for everyone.

1. Question authority

Mistakes happen. That's why a smart consumer reads credit card statements, bills and explanations of benefits very carefully.

For example, I saved a little over $65 by calling to find out why I was being charged a co-pay for a mammogram (which is fully covered under my insurance). The billing department's reaction was, more or less, "Whoops – sorry."

Probably the error would have been realized eventually and the money returned – but maybe not. Besides, why should I be deprived of the use of those dollars in the meantime?

Cell phones are vulnerable to a charming practice called "cramming," wherein a third-party biller sneaks unwanted charges onto an account. This happened to me; I was billed $19.99 for ringtone charges that I never ordered. Take a few minutes each month read your bill carefully.

Read your credit card bill line by line, too, to look for unauthorized charges. In an age of data breaches and card skimmers it's pretty easy for your information to be stolen. During a memorable two-month period in 2014 *three* of my cards were compromised.

Be vigilant

Credit expert and consumer advocate Beverly Harzog recommends you check your account activity regularly. While this won't keep fraud from happening, it helps you catch unauthorized charges early. Sometimes thieves make a small, unobtrusive charge, to see whether the card is still active or whether its owner is paying attention. Once the purchase is accepted, the crooks buy as much as possible before the card company notices an unfamiliar pattern of spending.

(Got a story there, too: Early one Saturday morning a card issuer's fraud department called to ask if I'd just tried to buy $18,000 worth of fire extinguishers in the United Kingdom. You couldn't make this stuff up if you tried.)

Debit card user? Be super-ultra-careful, then. If thieves get your card they can charge up a storm by specifying "credit" at the register. Within two to three days those transactions will show up – and maybe drain your bank account dry. It can take the bank or credit union weeks to investigate and give back the cash. Your landlord and/or creditors won't want to wait that long.

Whether credit or debit, check your account regularly. If you ever see a charge you don't recognize, call your financial institution *immediately*.

2. Game the drugstores

Back in the mid- to late 2000s it was possible to get multiple items for free or nearly free every week at CVS, Walgreens and Rite Aid. When I wrote about the topic for MSN Money, the headline was "Free Toothpaste For Life!" At times it seemed this really was the case; every couple of months I'd take at least two bags of toothpaste, shampoo, body wash and other items to a Seattle food bank.

These days the pickings are slimmer but they do exist, especially around Black Friday. Savvy shoppers can still get over-the-counter meds, toiletries, baby stuff, food items, cleaning supplies and more at excellent prices and sometimes for free.

Coupon and deal bloggers match the deals at drugstores the way they do at supermarkets. These involve "stacking" coupons with sale prices and points or scrip from each store's program (Register Rewards at Walgreens, ExtraBucks at CVS and Plenti at Rite Aid).

Paying little to nothing for household needs can be a huge boost to your budget. Keep in mind, though, that stores wouldn't do this if it cost them money. That's why a smart shopper pays attention to the hidden dangers of these programs:

- Loss leaders pull you in, but you might be tempted by things that *aren't* on sale.
- The points/scrip have expiration dates so if you don't use it, you lose it.
- Speaking of losing: If your rewards blow away (I've found them in parking lots) or disappear to the bottom of your purse or backpack, there go your savings.

Done right, these programs *rock*. Suppose you pay $5 for something and get $5 in rewards. Apply it toward another freebie on your next trip, or use the scrip as a head start on something you needed anyway.

Getting started

The reality show "Extreme Couponing" gave Q-users a bad name for a while. We all looked like lunatic hoarders after average viewers got a look at garages full of mustard and cereal. But the impact of the show has faded, and now we can get back to the business of stretching our dollars without fear of public censure.

New to the Q? Don't dive in too fast. If you're fortunate enough to live in a town with all three drugstore chains (or even two), start slowly. Coupon savants suggest focusing on one store at a time, to familiarize yourself with the ads and the rewards program.

Learn the store's coupon policy, too. In fact, some couponistas suggest printing it out to show to new cashiers who don't understand the rules.

As your confidence grows, add other stores. However, don't let deal-seeking overtake your life. If you're spending multiple hours and/or driving miles out of your way to get one or two things for free, you're doing it wrong.

Shop early in the week, since some of these deals sell out quickly. Dealistas say that Sunday mornings are best, before all the other coupon hounds descend.

If an advertised product is missing, politely ask an employee to check the stockroom. A drugstore manager once told me he puts just a few out at a time so that *all* customers – rather than just "the coupon ladies" – have a shot at the week's deals.

Tips from the pros

About those stockpiles: Remember that shelters can use all the toiletries you want to donate. Perhaps a friend who's also having tough times would appreciate that bottle of body wash or a two-pack of toothbrushes. You can frame this as, "You won't *believe* what I got for free! And since we've already got a ton of [whatever], I hope you can use these."

These items make great stocking stuffers, too. I once interviewed a woman who collected free lotion, razors, hair-care items and other toiletries all year long to make "grown-up Christmas stockings" for her adult kids. The boxes were a huge hit, she said, because they gave her children's budgets a little breathing room.

A few more tactics:

Curate those credits. Put your store scrip with the coupons you're using, or rubber-band them to your debit/credit card. Don't let it expire!

Split an order. The rewards are for "your next purchase." Savvy couponers pay for one or two products that give rewards, then use that scrip to pay for the rest of the stuff in their carts. (That *is* your next purchase, right?)

Check clearance bins. Store credit goes further this way. Sometimes items are slightly damaged – *very* slightly, e.g., a corner of the package got torn. Remember, you can still use manufacturer coupons on damaged items.

Be flexible. So you normally use Crest but the Colgate is free this week. Is there even a question?

Step back. If the store is really hectic and you're not in a rush, don't hit the register until things have quieted down. Or if you're in line with a dozen coupons and store scrip, let the folks with just one item go ahead of you. It'll take you a little longer but think of the karma points you'll earn! And unlike rewards programs, karma points have no expiration date.

3. Hack Amazon

The online juggernaut rules the hearts (and wallets) of millions due to its huge selection, low prices, constantly changing deals, attentive customer service, and fast or even free delivery.

As noted above, you can get Amazon gift cards through Swagbucks and MyPoints. The following tactics will help you stretch that virtual scrip much, much further.

Buy locally. You might not have to order online at all because some stores – including but not limited to Wal-Mart, Best Buy, Staples and Target – will match Amazon's prices as long as it's the identical item and currently in stock. This would let you save your Amazon GCs for another time.

Aim for the threshold. Shipping is free to the Lower 48 if you buy $35 or more at a time. Bummer for you if you're not an Amazon Prime member and your order is $34.84, amirite? Head for a site like FillerItemsFinder.com or FillerChecker.com and select an item that costs just enough to push you into Free Shipping Territory. If you're just 16 cents shy of not having to pay for shipping, it doesn't matter whether you actually need Genova 52117 Tubing Plastic.

Check for cash-back. Certain categories on Amazon can be accessed through cash-back shopping sites. Search online for "cash-back shopping Amazon."

Get help from a pro. Sites like Jungle Deals And Steals, CamelCamelCamel and The Tracktor provide all sorts of services for Amazon shoppers, including but not limited to deal alerts, price tracking and notable price drops. You can specify Amazon-only or all-sellers deals, and choose to include used or refurbished items. At least one, CamelCamelCamel, lets you import your Amazon wish list so you'll get the best price (a big help during the holidays).

Check the price. So you've found an item on Amazon that you think is super-affordable. To be sure, use a tool called PriceJump (http://www.savings.com/pricejump). Copy and paste the Amazon URL and the tracker compares the item's cost with those at 5,000 other online retailers and also local stores.

Use coupons. Visit one of the price-comparison websites mentioned earlier in this chapter and type "Amazon" into the search box. Codes for price breaks, free shipping or free-gift-with purchase should pop up. The retailer has its own coupons, too, at http://www.amazon.com/Coupons/b?ie=UTF8&node=223135201 1.

4. Pay creatively

When it's time to ante up, think outside the (payment) envelope. You could save money with some or all of the following tactics:

Ask for a discount. A relative got two estimates for tree stump removal, then asked the company she preferred to match the other's (slightly lower) quote. The manager agreed. You might also request a price break for using cash instead of credit for a medical co-pay or auto-repair deductible; I got 5 percent off some major dental work that way.

Haggle. A time-honored way of bringing costs down! Practice saying, "Is that your best price?" or "I'm tempted by this purchase but I'd buy right now if you could offer me a discount." Sometimes a manager will surprise you.

Pay the full premium. Vehicle insurance is generally cheaper if you pay by the year or half-year rather than month to month. Expect annual savings of $17 to $82. Also on the subject of auto insurance, you could...

Drive selectively. Some companies give insurance price breaks if you use the vehicle during off-peak hours and/or log fewer miles. Get yourself some quotes.

Use layaway. Generally speaking this isn't the greatest idea because your buying power is then limited to one store. However, desperate times call for desperate measures: If you don't have the money all at once, layaway might be what makes a holiday happen at your house.

Barter. Got something to trade? Make it work for you! See if the veterinarian needs someone to clean the office. Ask whether the piano teacher would trade lessons for fresh produce from your garden. Keep in mind that bartering may have tax ramifications. See "Bartering Income" on the Internal Revenue Service website, https://www.irs.gov/taxtopics/tc420.html.

Trade with friends. Why rent that power washer when your buddy owns one – especially if your SkilSaw would make his deck project a lot easier? The possibilities are limited only by your imagination. Well, that and by the stuff you and your friends have. I call this The Pickup Truck Theory of Life: "You don't need to own a truck – you just need to know someone who owns a truck."

5. Grocery-shop with intention

It's so, *so* easy to get sidetracked at the supermarket. The fragrance of freshly baked chocolate chip cookies. Out-of-season fruit in mouthwatering displays. Free samples of pricey cheeses or gourmet salsa so tasty that you find yourself adding a jar to the shopping cart. (Hint: Stores wouldn't give stuff away if it didn't regularly lead to purchases.)

A tactic I call "goal-oriented groceries" will help keep you from running amok in the aisles. Start your shopping list with a personal goal, written in capital letters and preferably with a black Sharpie so that it can't be ignored. Partway down the list, repeat the goal or write down another one. Repeat as needed.

An example:

RETIRE BY 35

Milk

Store-brand multigrain bread (coupon in circular)

One pound dry beans

BUILD EMERGENCY FUND

Apples

Chicken thighs (value pack because it's on sale)

Peanut butter

PAY OFF CONSUMER DEBT

Potatoes

One pound ground beef

Eggs

STAY UNDER BUDGET

Oatmeal from bulk bin

Monterey jack cheese

Lentils

RETIRE BY 35 – SERIOUSLY!!!!

Kinda hard to ignore those goals, huh? Which is entirely the point: Each time you see those all-cap exhortations you'll be reminded of the reason(s) why you're shopping so carefully. Dollars spent on high-end meats or tomatoes flown in from Israel are dollars you can't put toward a long-term goal.

Suppose you could cut your food bills by $100 (or more) per month. What could that $1,200 (or more) per year do for the bottom line?

6. Look for better rates

When it comes to saving money, pick the lowest-hanging fruit first. A survey from Insurance.com compared the per-minute value of tactics such as changing cellphone carriers, carefully pricing new vehicles and seeking a better car insurance rate.

Shopping for insurance won quite handily, with a value of $54 per minute. A cynic would call that pretty convenient, since Insurance.com has an auto-insurance rate comparison tool. But consumers generally *can* benefit by using a tool like this every so often.

In part that's because a change in circumstances – reaching the age of 25, getting married, moving, taking a job with a shorter commute, even improving your credit score – can mean better rates. But it's also because even reasonably intelligent people wind up overpaying from the get-go and fail to do anything about it. (Ask me how I know.)

Too, this is *annual* gain. Dollars saved on things like car insurance, a cellphone plan or television/Internet service represent a continuing impact on the bottom line. For example, getting $100 off a smartphone is a sweet deal but those surveyed by Insurance.com saved an average of $179.28 *per year* by getting a better plan.

Just as you make time to exercise, give your budget a workout now and then. Suppose you really could save hundreds (or thousands) a year on your cable or cellphone plan – or, yes, on your car insurance. Think about that money being used toward consumer debt, an emergency fund or a retirement plan, instead of just being spent needlessly each year. Talk about opportunity cost.

7. Shop the dollar store

Although these one-buck emporia have come under fire for dangerous products like tainted toothpaste and poisonous pet products, there *are* ways that the dollar store can safely boost your budget.

Don't believe me? Maybe you'd believe Consumer Reports, which noted that the stores are fun, convenient and full of hot deals: "If you haven't been to a dollar store lately, prepare to be surprised."

Not every one is a "true" dollar store, however. Dollar Tree and 99 Cents Only are, because everything is $1 or less, whereas Dollar General and Family Dollar have $1 products but also many items that cost more. You may also see independent stores in your area, some of which have great deals and some of which are crammed with dismal goods.

Be judicious in your selection and you'll get name-brand housewares, toiletries, accessories and even foods at a considerable discount. The 99 Cents Only stores in particular can be a great place to shop since they have fresh produce along with frozen foods and dry goods.

Stick with the name-brand products and you should be fine. I've purchased lip balm, dental floss, soap, lotion, Epsom salts, cotton swabs and generic Benadryl this way. (That allergy med cost a penny per tablet, by the way. Can't beat that.) Steer clear of name-brand candy, though – many are actually smaller packages than those in other stores, so the rate is the same or worse.

Bonus: Since Dollar General, Dollar Tree and Family Dollar accept manufacturer coupons, you could wind up spending a lot less than a buck. In fact, you might not spend anything at all: The Coupon Mom blog has noted weeks when a dozen or more products were completely free after coupons. These weren't no-name items, either, but rather products from Johnson & Johnson, Alka-Seltzer, Colgate, Cover Girl, Triaminic, Hall's and Crest.

Note: Some dollar stores have their own coupons on their websites, Facebook pages or Twitter feeds.

Other dollar deals

Party and holiday supplies abound at dollar stores, although if you're on a tight budget you might want to put available celebration funds towards things like food and gifts.

When it comes to housewares, how much do you want to pay for a drain stopper or a mop bucket? I've saved a ton going to the dollar vs. department store for stuff like shelf liners, wooden clothespins, potholders, dish towels, sponges, bath mats and a laundry bag. And I'm still using a dollar-store strainer that my daughter gave me a dozen years ago.

The dollar store is a huge budgetary boost for homeschoolers or those in charge of scout troops or Sunday-school classes.

Workbooks, flash cards, bulletin board items, stickers, art supplies, stencils, puzzles and devotional books are – you guessed it – a buck. (If you're shopping at a true dollar store, that is.)

My own favorite dollar-store purchase: a three-pack of Hanes Her Way women's underwear. Yes, I admit it: I bought dollar-store skivvies. At 33 cents a pair, wouldn't you?

4: Finding Short-Term Help

Sometimes we need to ask for assistance. Not fun. I don't know anyone who turns handsprings at the chance to stand in a food bank line or to fill out applications for rent assistance.

This isn't the end of the world – even though it may feel that way. You're in a very tight spot that you can't wish yourself out of, but you *will* get through this. Naturally it would be better not to have to ask for help. Sometimes it's necessary.

This could be true even if you're not currently in crisis. Suppose that the money coming in right now more or less covers the money going out. Any household that's *just about* making it from month to month will eventually have the props kicked out from under. Count on it. A simple childhood illness or the need for minor auto repair can knock the whole house of cards flat. (Especially since there's really no such thing as "minor" car trouble.)

In order to improve your life you have to survive long enough to make significant changes. You can't do that if you're hungry, overdrawn at the bank or, heaven forbid, evicted.

Self-sufficiency is great, until you're looking at an empty cupboard or a shut-off notice. Please don't let pride get in the way of survival. Public and private entities exist to help during the lean times – and keep in mind that some are funded with your tax dollars.

When things get better, you can give back. Until then, do what you must to keep your household afloat.

The following tactics will turn barely-getting-by into a much more stable existence. Take it from someone who knows:

Sometimes transforming your life means getting a temporary utility break or taking a bag of staples from the food bank.

Getting started

The world of social services can be tough to navigate because, well, bureaucracy. Each agency may have its own set of rules and requirements. Lines or telephone wait times can be very long. There may not be enough help out there to see you through – and in some regions there may be little to no help at all.

More to the point, having to ask for help can really body-slam your self-esteem, especially if the process seems intrusive. And it almost certainly will. You'll have to explain some potentially uncomfortable things – stuff like your marital status, how long it's been since you worked and the fact that although you're due child support your ex has never paid it.

These people are not giving you a hard time. They are doing their jobs. Agencies need to put everyone through the same paces. Try not to take it personally, and remember: This too shall pass.

Looking for help in all the right places

The first thing you need is some paper, a notebook, a Word document or anything that will let you record information. For each phone call you make – and there will probably be lots of them – you need to take careful, specific notes.

For example, suppose new food bank clients can apply only between 10 a.m. and noon in your town. Suppose also that there's *always* a line and it takes two business days to process an application. Finding this out ahead of time will keep you from showing up on a Friday afternoon and expecting to be sent home with food.

You'll also be making lists of the things you need when applying for help at each agency – including but not limited to birth certificates, government-issued ID, rent receipt, or current utility bill or something else bearing your address. (Pop quiz: Could you lay your hands on your birth certificate right now? How about your children's?)

An essential number

The first thing to write in your notebook is "211." This community services clearinghouse is run by the United Way and is available in most of the country. Those three digits can direct you toward all sorts of assistance. Dial it and start talking to whoever answers.

Be *very* specific about your situation, e.g., "My rent is paid only through the end of this month" or "There's not much food in my fridge and I have two children." Then contact every agency that the 211 worker suggests, even if you don't think it's a match. You might be surprised. (For example, you don't have to be Catholic to get help from Catholic Social Services.)

As you talk to each agency, be sure to ask this question: ***"Do you know of any other organizations that might be able to help?"*** Those in the community service field sometimes hear about aid sources that fly under 211's radar: a church that offers rent assistance, say, or a service organization that serves free lunch to seniors five days a week.

Speaking up for yourself

Yes, it can be hard to say, "I need help – and fast." Say it anyway. **You must be your own advocate.**

Things you need won't magically appear. Aid workers are not mind-readers, and they probably don't have time to pry specific information from you – the people on hold or behind you in line need help, too.

The process doesn't have to be demeaning. Frame it as, "I'm in a tough spot after my illness/layoff/divorce and I'm trying to get back on my feet. Can you help me?"

Besides, these folks have heard it all before. They're not looking down on you. Their job is to help.

If there were a way to make this easier I would happily provide it. But there's no simple, single tactic to get all your needs met the same day you ask. In fact, it may take days and days of calling. No matter how exhausting this feels, it's essential that you keep going.

Finally: ***Believe the part about getting back on your feet***. You will – but that means doing the hard, necessary work of looking for help right now.

5: Staying Healthy

It's essential to have some kind of health insurance. Depending on your income you might not pay at all for coverage through the healthcare marketplace.

That doesn't mean your troubles are over, however. In some cases (including my own) "affordable" insurance amounts basically to catastrophic coverage. That's because the deductible is so high that we're wary about seeking any medical care other than the paid-for annual exam.

This isn't always a bad thing. Going to the doctor for every little sniffle may contribute to the over-prescription of antibiotics. Years ago I routinely visited the doctor for upper-respiratory issues because I had great insurance. These days I have a wait-and-see attitude to go along with my $1,700 deductible.

Were I to experience fevers or steadily worsening pain it would be a different story. Although I cringe to think of having to meet that deductible, the fact is that I have an emergency fund that would cover the costs *if necessary*. Not everyone is in that position.

Maybe that's you right now. Would treatment be affordable for your household? What if you don't have dental insurance and you develop serious jaw pain? Or suppose your kid can't see the blackboard and you don't have a vision plan?

This chapter contains workarounds for folks who can't afford to use the insurance unless it's truly an emergency. It's also helpful to people who, for whatever reason, don't have any coverage at all.

Care on a sliding scale

Nationwide, more than 8,500 **federally qualified health centers** (http://findahealthcenter.hrsa.gov/Search_HCC.aspx) provide health care based on your ability to pay. This includes prenatal care, sick visits, annual checkups, and ongoing care for babies and children. Some of these places also offer oral health, substance abuse, mental health and vision treatment.

State public health clinics (http://www.cdc.gov/mmwr/international/relres.html) provide varying degrees of basic care. Depending on where you live, you can receive ongoing general health care, immunizations (including flu shots), family planning/pregnancy testing, well-child exams, mental health services and testing for sexually transmitted diseases.

The National Association of Free & Charitable Clinics (http://www.nafcclinics.org/clinics/search) offers links to more than 1,200 free and low-cost healthcare providers around the country. You might find one in your area.

Call 211 and ask if any free or inexpensive care options exist in your region. For example, a Seattle social services agency called North Helpline hosts two clinics per week, one of them free to the uninsured and the other operating on a sliding scale basis. Maybe something like that operates in your area, too, but you won't know unless you ask.

Investigate all these options *before* you need them, vs. waiting until you're flattened by a bad back or a really bad case of the flu. The first time you use places like this might feel odd, especially if you're accustomed to being seen at a private practice. Swallow your pride and get yourself an appointment. You owe it to yourself and your family to stay healthy. Besides, state and federal health clinics are funded with tax dollars so you've already helped pay for them.

Finding cheaper treatment

It's possible to bargain-hunt for medical care. Sites like **Fair Health Consumer** (http://fairhealthconsumer.org) and **Healthcare Bluebook** (https://healthcarebluebook.com) crunch treatment numbers to come up with what it generally costs to get medical care in different parts of the country. **New Choice Health** (http://www.newchoicehealth.com/) also has pricing information and lets you request a quote directly from medical facilities in your area.

This matters. For example, lab work costs vary widely depending on where it's done. Be honest with your doctor, e.g., "I've been out of work for six months. Can you write down the exact info for this blood work (or whatever) so I can go home and look for the most affordable option?"

Embarrassing? A little, maybe. Consumer-savvy? Definitely. Obviously this won't work for an emergency situation, but if you have the luxury of even a day or two to research treatment costs, then do so.

When you're uninsured

We're all supposed to have insurance now, but some people just don't. If that's you, then consider these two tactics:

At Healthcare Bluebook, type in what's needed (foot surgery, skin lesion biopsy, whatever) plus your zip code and get an idea of what you might pay for that treatment in your area. As the website notes, the cost for the same network procedure can vary by up to 400 percent. Even if you do have insurance, using a tool like could mean having to fork over less of a co-pay (e.g., 20 percent of $300 rather than $500).

Or use Fair Health Consumer's cost lookup tool to get an idea of what an average service or treatment should be, then print out something called a "binding cost estimate." This basically says,

"This amount is what we know to be less than a billed charge but more than a typical insurance payout."

Present it to a potential provider, say frankly that cost is a huge issue for your household and you'd like to know if you could get the needed treatment at this price.

Why would anyone agree to take less than the standard cost? Because you'd be paying a little more than an insurance company would, and you'd be doing so immediately vs. requiring a claim to be filed.

Offer to pay in full at the time of the visit. If you can pay in cash, say so – it might be enough of an incentive to get the provider to agree. Even if you had to use a credit card you'd at least be getting the best possible price for treatment.

Again: This is one of the reasons to have an emergency fund. See Chapter 11 for some amazing – and amazingly easy – savings hacks.

Do you need a hospital?

Read your insurance policy to learn which hospital(s) the provider prefers. If you've just been hit by a truck, the paramedics will want to take you to the closest emergency room – and you should let them! But if you slip and fall on an icy sidewalk or take a spill during a bike ride, you have the luxury of choice. Be sure to choose a preferred provider.

However, you may not need to head for the ER. Say you twist an ankle during a softball game or develop a fever and cough on a Saturday night. Such issues could likely be handled by an urgent care clinic. Some are staffed with nurse practitioners and others have full-fledged medical doctors.

Either way, these "doc in the box" centers cost less and you'll probably get examined faster there than you would at a busy ER. In some cases you won't be charged if it turns out they can't treat your issue and want to refer you to a physician. Again, it pays to know in advance which urgent care facilities are on your insurance provider's preferred list.

Women's health issues

Medicare, Medicaid and most insurance programs cover the cost of mammograms and Pap smears in full. Here are some options for the un- or underinsured:

American Breast Cancer Foundation. Grants are available to pay for diagnostic treatment. To find out if you qualify, call 844-219-2223 (toll-free).

National Mammography Program (http://www.nationalbreastcancer.org/nbcf-programs/patient-services). Free mammograms and diagnostic breast care services, plus continued treatment after abnormal test results or cancer diagnosis.

NBCCED. The National Breast and Cervical Cancer Early Detection Program (https://nccd.cdc.gov/dcpc_Programs/index.aspx#/1) provides free or low-cost screening to eligible women. Part of the Centers for Disease Control and Prevention, it also offers services such as HPV tests, pelvic exams and further testing and referrals if necessary.

Susan G. Komen Foundation. Check the organization's website (http://ww5.komen.org/affiliates.aspx), or call 877-465-6636 (toll-free) to find low-cost mammography options in your region.

The YWCA (http://www.ywca.org). Free cervical cancer screenings and mammograms are available in some parts of the United States.

Planned Parenthood (http://www.plannedparenthood.org). Women's health exams – including but not limited to birth control, cervical cancer screenings, and pelvic and breast exams – are available on a sliding scale basis. You can get referrals to and information on low- and no-cost mammograms.

Local sources. Try doing a search for "free mammograms/Pap smears [your city]." You might discover options that don't show up anywhere else.

Keeping prescription costs down

Maintenance meds and short-term drug regimens alike can take a huge bite out of your healthcare budget. Some insurance plans include mail-order pharmacy privileges, which can save you some money.

But not always. When I switched insurance plans I was paying $4 a month for generic maintenance meds, so I sent both prescriptions off to the mail-order pharmacy. One came in at $8 for three months' worth. The other cost me more than $29 for 90 days. Whoops. Learn from my mistake: Read the generic medications list *very* carefully.

Even if you're not on maintenance meds, the cost of curing even a simple illness can be surprisingly high. Use one or more of the following tips to get the most for your healthcare dollars.

Common meds may be free. Some supermarket pharmacies offer certain antibiotics, generic Lipitor, prenatal and children's vitamins, the diabetes drug Metformin and other medications without charge. Among the grocery chains providing free medications are Amigos United, Giant Eagle, Meijer, Price Chopper, Publix, Reasor's, Schnucks, ShopRite and Wegman's.

Ask for help. A certain number of discounted or even free drugs are available for those on extremely limited incomes. You can apply for assistance through groups like NeedyMeds (http://www.needymeds.org/), the Chronic Disease Fund (http://www.mygooddays.org/) and the Partnership for Prescription Assistance (https://www.pparx.org/).

Go generic. Wal-Mart first offered $4 prescriptions a decade ago and other stores and pharmacies jumped on the bandwagon. Use a site called MedTipster.com to find generic equivalents of the drugs you need, whether maintenance or short-term, and then check the formularies for local stores offering $4 scripts.

There's an app for that. Sites like GoodRx.com and LowestMed.com let you compare prescription costs in your area.

Split pills. If you need a 10-mg drug, it could be possible to buy 20-mg pills for about the same price, then use a pill-splitter to halve them. Note: You *must* ask your provider about this, since not all drugs can be safely divided.

About online pharmacies

Even if you don't have a mail-order pharmacy associated with your insurance plan, it's still possible to buy online. Due diligence is necessary, however, since some Internet drugstores are bogus. The Mayo Clinic website notes that in some cases prescriptions have "turned out to contain no active ingredient or to contain the wrong medicine."

It is illegal to ship non-FDA-approved drugs into the United States. You should order only from online pharmacies in the U.S. Although some people think it's safe to use Canadian virtual pharmacies, the National Association of Boards of Pharmacy notes that some rogue northerners source their drugs from countries where standards may be lax and counterfeit pills more common.

To find an approved source, run the pharmacy's name through LegitScript.com.

Get a flu shot

If you don't believe in flu shots, please don't stop reading this chapter. Just skip this section and move on. I'm not naïve enough to think I can change your mind in a couple of sentences, so I won't try. However, I want to make sure you read the other money-saving techniques that occur in the rest of this chapter.

Personally, I think the flu shot is a good idea for most people. Those of us with insurance, even crappy insurance, can get immunized for free. Anyone who can't should check the following workarounds.

Public health. Find your state's health department at http://www.cdc.gov/mmwr/international/relres.html, then look for public health clinics that immunize. Depending on your current finances, you might not have to pay.

Federally qualified health centers. Another income-based option; find one near you at http://findahealthcenter.hrsa.gov/Search_HCC.aspx.

Vaccines for Children program

(http://www.cdc.gov/vaccines/programs/vfc/contacts-state.html). More than 44,000 doctors nationwide offer free immunizations for children under 19 if they are uninsured, underinsured, Medicaid-eligible or American Indian/Alaska Native. Although some doctors charge to administer the shot, your child cannot be turned away if you can't afford to pay the fee.

Medicare. The senior health program covers flu shots – no co-pay, no deductible.

Non-medical sites. The vaccine is offered at workplaces, schools, houses of worship, and Women Infant Children nutrition programs. Flu shots also pop up at random public events, so do a search for "flu shots [your city]" and call 211 to ask for upcoming immunization options. Again, you may not have to pay full price, or at all.

Open (your wallet) wide?

Both Healthcare Bluebook and Fair Health Consumer provide info on dental care as well. In fact, a Consumer Reports survey indicates that people who use those sites to ask their dentists for price breaks are generally successful.

Those discounts may be essential because not everyone has dental insurance – and some dental insurance isn't worth much. Twice-annual cleanings and an X-ray every couple of years plus a portion of fillings and a (smaller) portion of crowns and other services are about the best some of us can expect.

For that reason, some consumer advocates think dental insurance isn't worth it – that instead you should set aside the premiums and use them to pay for the most affordable cleanings you can find. My suggestion is to do the math. If dental care is expensive in your region and you plan to get two cleanings a year (and you should!), dental insurance might be cost-effective. It has been for me.

Investigate discount dental plans, too. You pay an annual fee (generally between $80 and $200) for access to dentists who offer discounts of as much as 50 percent. This is not a scam; Consumer Reports mentioned it in a list of dental care options, and noted that 60 percent of U.S. dentists belong to such networks. Learn more at http://www.dentalplans.com.

Fewer dentists belong to "dental HMO" plans, but they're a pretty good deal if you can get them. Your $200 to $300 annual fee gets you semi-annual cleanings and exams for no extra charge plus considerable discounts on fillings, root canals and crowns. Only about 20 percent of U.S. dentists are associated with these plans; to check availability in your region, visit http://www.nadp.org/about/cdorganization.aspx.

Other dental options

University dental schools offer inexpensive (or even free) care. Yes, they're students – but they're about to become dentists, and their work is supervised. To locate schools in your region, visit the **National Institute of Dental and Craniofacial Research** website (http://www.nidcr.nih.gov/) and click on "Finding Dental Care."

As noted previously, the **National Association of Free & Charitable Clinics** (http://www.nafcclinics.org/clinics/search) has links to free and low-cost health care that sometimes includes oral health programs.

Free dentistry clinics or short-term events pop up now and then. At one such event in my own city people camped out overnight to ensure they'd get care. Check a site called **Free Dental Work** (http://www.freedentalcare.us/) for possibilities, and also search for **"free dental work [your city]."**

Finally, a nonprofit called **Dentistry From The Heart** (www.dentistryfromtheheart.org) works to link pro bono practitioners with patients who need care.

Regular cleanings are important, both to forestall gum disease (which can lead to tooth loss and other serious health issues if left untreated) and also to spot other potential problems. **Some dental hygiene schools offer low-cost care**; visit the American Dental Hygienists Association website (http://www.adha.org/dental-hygiene-programs) to look for possibilities in your region.

Straight talk for teeth

Braces aren't just about looks. According to the Mayo Clinic the way we bite, chew and even speak has a lot to do with whether our teeth and jaws are properly aligned. In addition, correctly aligned teeth are easier to clean and floss, which helps prevent decay and gum disease.

Plenty of households have health insurance but no dental coverage. Not all dental insurance applies to orthodontics. Fortunately, lower-cost (sometimes *much* lower) options exist.

Those with extremely low incomes might be eligible for programs such as **Smile For A Lifetime** (http://www.s4l.org/Default.aspx) and **Smiles Change Lives** (http://smileschangelives.org). Note: Each program has different qualifications and since need outstrips supply, your child may not be accepted. It also takes time to be approved, so be patient.

Members of the **American Association of Orthodontists** provide care to low-income children who qualify. Visit https://www.mylifemysmile.org/#dos to find out how to apply.

The AAO also has a list of **dental schools with orthodontics programs** at https://www.aaomembers.org/Education/Accredited-Schools.cfm. Such care isn't free but will certainly be cheaper than an orthodontics practice. Note that some of these schools accept Medicaid-authorized cases, and that a child with a particularly unusual case could receive care for free.

Discount dental plans (see above). Not all discount dental plans include orthodontic care, but if yours does the savings can be considerable. A man I interviewed for MSN Money reported saving more than $3,000 this way. Note: Before you actually buy the plan, be sure to verify that member orthodontists are accepting new patients.

Don't skip the dentist

Due to a combination of family issues and lack of funds, I went without dental care from ages 16 to 20 and ages 21 to 24. Untreated cavities ultimately led to a serious abscess, several root canals and the loss of two molars.

That didn't have to happen. I hope you won't let it happen to you. Please use the tactics noted above to get some basic care. Twice-annual cleanings and occasional X-rays can save you a literal world of hurt later on.

About those films: Depending on your age and the current health of your teeth, you may be able to go two to three years between bitewing X-rays. Before you think, "Forget it – I can't afford X-rays, period," let me suggest that you can't afford *not* to get them. Cavities can develop between teeth or beneath an existing filling. Dentists and dental hygienists don't have X-ray vision, which is why they have X-ray machines.

As an example, I give you the story of a relatively young patient seen by my dental-hygienist sister. The woman didn't have insurance and as a result never got X-rays.

Until one of her teeth started hurting, that is, at which point the film showed decay too deep to repair. The recommended treatment cost more than $1,000. A preventive bitewing X-ray would have cost $55.

Looking for affordable (preferably free) dental care can be tiring. Please do it anyway. Prevention is cheaper than repair. Take it from me: It also hurts a lot less than an abscess.

The eyes have it

According to the Centers for Disease Control and Prevention, only 58 percent of Americans with private health insurance have packages with vision coverage. Those of us without it can feel tempted to ignore the headaches our old glasses give us. What's harder to ignore is the teacher's note that says your son or daughter has been squinting to read the blackboard.

If that's you and you can't afford eye care for your children, investigate one or more of these programs:

Vision USA (http://www.aoafoundation.org/vision-usa/), which operates in 40 states and the District of Columbia, organizes members of the American Optometric Association to treat patients who can't afford eye care.

Sight For Students (http://www.sightforstudents.org) focuses on eye care (exams, glasses) for uninsured low-income students. The student must be under 18 and not yet a high-school graduate.

Depending on the state, the **Children's Health Insurance Program** (http://www.insurekidsnow.gov/state/index.html) may provide free or reduced-cost eye exams for youths up to age 19.

New Eyes (http://www.aao.org/eyecare-america) offers eyeglass vouchers to people who have already had exams. The nonprofit works through social service agencies, doctors, healthcare advocates and places of worship; you must have someone from one of those groups submit an application for you.

Paying less for specs

Consumer Reports says the best price/service combo can be found at Costco. You don't have to be a member to take advantage of their vision services.

Eye-care chains often run coupon specials. Watch the Sunday inserts or visit a site like Savings.com or RetailMeNot.com to look for coupons.

If your prescription isn't too complicated, check out online eyeglass emporia such as Eyeglasses.com, Glasses Shop, Glasses.com and GlassesSpot.com. These virtual optical shops offer some amazing deals, e.g., frames starting at $6.95.

Follow these sites on Facebook because they sometimes post specials or discount codes. When you decide to buy, access the retailer through a cash-back shopping site for rebates of up to 12 percent plus proprietary coupons.

Be proactive

Generally speaking, good health doesn't just happen to you. It's important to take the right steps to keep yourself in the pink.

Eat as well as you can on what you have. The Internet is crammed with recipes that use simple, inexpensive ingredients. Or visit your local library for cookbooks that focus on money-saving meals.

Drink plenty of water. If your local water tastes blah, look for a filtration pitcher at the thrift store and shop online for the cheapest refill cartridges. Or doctor the tap water with a slice of lemon or lime. Can't afford fresh citrus? Get a box of Wyler's sugar-free lemonade packets from the dollar store and add a sprinkle to each glass or pitcher. (This works even on Philadelphia water.)

Exercise for physical and mental health. This could be as simple as walking around the block or up and down the apartment-house stairs. My daughter, who has a chronic illness, has found YouTube exercise videos geared toward people who can't do vigorous regimens but still want to get cardiovascular, strength or flexibility workouts.

Find cheap or free stress-relievers. Even 20 minutes listening to your favorite music or soaking in a hot bath can be a nice break from *what's-next?* mode. Laughter is a marvelous stress-buster, so visit the library for comedy DVDs or books by humorists. (If you've still got Internet at home, look for funny stuff online.)

Above all, pay attention to small health issues so they don't become big problems. When you're in financial crisis it's tempting to ignore your body's calls for help. A relative's husband ignored an infection and it landed him in the hospital on an antibiotic IV drip. Far better to go to the public health clinic than wind up in the emergency room.

6: How To Live Rent-Free
(Or At Least Cheaper Than You Are Now)

According to the 50-30-20 budget rule, no more than 50 percent of your after-tax income should be spent on shelter, food, utilities, clothing and insurance. Given how much it costs to rent or own a place to live, cutting the cost of housing is an excellent way to reduce spending in that 50-percent category.

This is particularly important if:

You're already living paycheck to paycheck.

You want to cut spending to the bone to meet a short-term goal, such as paying off consumer or education debt.

You've got a specific dream, like retiring early or starting your own business (or both!).

If you/someone in your household got laid off or were diagnosed with a serious illness, start looking at other housing options right away. Ideally you've already done so, as part of that financial fire drill. If not, get going. The time to look for housing help is *not* the day before your rent/mortgage is due.

Subsidized housing is an obvious tactic. Check to see if you meet the income requirements, but don't count on receiving a place right away. Waiting lists can be extremely long (think "years"). For federally subsidized housing, see http://portal.hud.gov/hudportal/HUD?src=/topics/rental_assistance . Some states have their own programs, so you should also visit http://portal.hud.gov/hudportal/HUD?src=/topics/rental_assistance /local.

Rent assistance may be available from groups such as the Salvation Army, the American Red Cross and Catholic Charities (again, you don't need to be Catholic). It might also be forthcoming from private foundations/charities or smaller religious groups; for example, the church I attended in Seattle gave out cash assistance.

As noted previously, when you call 211 or any other agency you need to be *very* specific about your situation, e.g., "My rent is due in two weeks and I am $100 short."

Stopgap measures

Crashing with family/friends. If you've got an extensive support network, you might be able to get by for quite a while by staying a week or two in each place (especially if you're house-sitting while a pal or cousin is on vacation). The nomad life is disruptive, but it can be done. Make your hosts glad to have you by walking the dog, running a load of laundry, cleaning the bathroom or cooking your famous spaghetti sauce.

Long-term crashing. Few of us really *want* to move back into our old bedrooms. But if your parents offer, consider taking them up on it. Draw up an agreement specifying how many hours a day you will look for work and that you are willing to do household chores and chip in for groceries. Later on, if you slip into dependent mode – letting Mom do your laundry, watching TV while Dad does yard work – the parents can use the document to snap you out of your torpor.

Emergency shelters. These vary from gym-mat-on-warehouse-floor to warm and comfortable family settings. While you might shudder at the possibility you still need to learn where they are. This is essential knowledge should you face eviction, have one of your couch-surfs fall through or get on the wrong side of a previously accommodating relative.

Living on your own (but not alone)

Shared housing. Want to leave a pricey apartment but don't want a dicey replacement? Start by asking around; someone might know someone who's looking for a roommate. Put out the word at grad school, your place of worship, your former sorority/fraternity or any other place compatible folks might be found.

Or check with the National Shared Housing Institute (http://nationalsharedhousing.org/), which has a directory of member organizations in 22 states and abroad. Bonus: You might be matched in a situation where you can work off some (or lots) of your rent, e.g., helping senior homeowners with chores. Such a price break would let you build up your emergency fund and figure out your next move.

Take in a roommate. Struggling to make your mortgage payment? Wondering why you thought that single you needed a two-bedroom apartment? A roomie or two can make a huge difference. While this could be tricky, you might also wind up making a new friend.

Or *start* with your friends – that is, let it be known among your besties that you've got a room for rent. Maybe one of them is secretly hankering to save money, too, and will jump at the chance to terminate that month-to-month lease and move in. Write up a rental agreement, even if you're rooming with your BFF; that way everyone's clear on house rules, rent due dates and the like.

Suppose no friends want to bunk with you? Look elsewhere. A few options:

- Social media – let it be known that you've got rooms to let
- If you get a part-time job, put the word out there (folks who get 30 hours or fewer per week may be looking to share)
- Put up a note at your place of worship

- The student housing/student life departments at area colleges/universities

Don't neglect due diligence, no matter where potential roomers are found. A site called Sharing Housing has a "housemate questionnaire," which makes a good worksheet for potential renters. Find it at https://www.sharinghousing.com/home-mate-compatibility-assessment-about/.

The site also has a section devoted to articles on finding good housemates. Scan these to avoid making mistakes like not checking references or allowing someone to move in even though he doesn't have all of the deposit in hand. (Hint: If he can't handle money now, what makes you think he'll be able to pay his rent on time?)

Become a house-sitter

Word of mouth is an easy way to start. I've gotten housesitting jobs in Los Angeles, Anchorage and Seattle simply by putting it out in the universe that I'm looking for a place to stay. Bonus: Sometimes I get paid in addition to getting a free flop.

But if you're looking at house-sitting as a long-term way of life, I recommend a trio of resources that have been around for decades:

- **The Caretaker Gazette** (http://caretaker.org/)
- **Workers on Wheels** (http://www.work-for-rvers-and-campers.com/)
- **Workamper News** (https://www.workamper.com/)

"Caretaking" can be as simple as picking up the mail and watering the plants but it can also mean a full-time job caring for animals and/or a landscape. Obviously you need to have good references; with some jobs it helps to have certain skills, such as experience with horses or the ability to make minor repairs.

"Workamping" means you'll be putting in at least part-time hours while living in a recreational vehicle. That's usually in a campground but sometimes involves caring for private property.

Insist on a written contract. One woman I interviewed was not told she would have to pay the utilities (in Florida, in the summer). Another house-sitter was surprised to learn that several large dogs lived in the home.

Be ready to run

You also need an exit strategy. Don't spend your last dime traveling to a housesitting or caretaking job only to find out you've been misled. Suppose you are cash-poor and couldn't afford to keep the central air running during August in Miami? Or that you're not comfortable with dogs and *certainly* not comfortable with having to walk them and clean up after them?

Don't feel bad about backing out if the conditions under which you agreed to work were changed with no notice. But *do* have a place to go, and sufficient cash to get yourself there.

All this isn't meant to scare you off, but rather to make sure you approach this with wide-open eyes. Housesitting can actually work quite well. Right after the recession I spoke with a woman who landed in a long-term housesitting job after losing her job and her apartment. She wound up healthier than she'd been in years because she had to mow the lawn and do other landscaping chores, vs. sitting at a desk for nine hours a day.

I've also interviewed workampers who love the chance to visit different parts of the country without paying for space rent. My favorite story, though, was the man who landed in a beautiful home in a ski resort. All he had to do was clear out for two weeks a year, so the wealthy owner could spend the holidays there. Maybe you'll be that lucky.

Look for a rent-free gig

In other words, exchange care or skills for room and board. Start in your own family circle or that of a close friend. Suppose Grandma and Grandpa want to stay out of the nursing home but the extended family can't afford help with daily living chores? Offer to move in and do some of the shopping, cooking, cleaning and yard work.

Notice I said *some* – don't let other family members dump it all on you. You may need a place to live but they cannot expect you to be on call 24/7. In fact, you need to arrange for two days off a week, during which other relatives (or paid help) can step in. Remember: Full-time care would cost a bundle, so you'd be saving the family a lot of money by living there.

Good with children? Maybe a friend or relative with young children will give you a place to stay in return for a certain number of hours of babysitting per week. Or check the "live-in nanny" ads.

Strong and caring? Look into a job as a live-in personal care attendant for people with health issues or as a general factotum for an elderly person who wants to remain in the home but needs some help. You'll need stellar references for this one, too, so start lining them up now.

Handy folks might be able to land spots as apartment house managers. I did this job myself and it can be frustrating at times – say, at 2 a.m. when a drunken tenant rings the doorbell to say he's lost his keys. But not having to pay rent each month is *huge*.

In a larger apartment complex you might not even need to be handy. Instead, you'll spend your time doing paperwork and showing apartments, and delegating the clogged sinks to a superintendent.

If all this sounds complicated, that's because it is. It will likely take a ton of phone work and of putting yourself out there – and maybe even humbling yourself, if you always vowed you'd never move back in with your folks.

Keep at it. Securing housing can take time – maybe *lots* of time – so don't let shame or embarrassment paralyze you. Wait until the last minute and you just might find yourself standing on the sidewalk with a suitcase and nowhere to go.

7: Getting Dressed On A Dime

My number-one frugal tip? Stay out of the stores.

While I'm not saying that you should never go shopping again, I challenge you to think about how much you really need. Do members of your household have sufficient clothing to get from washday to washday? Does it fit properly? Is it in good repair?

As the old saying goes, "Enough is as good as a feast." Sartorially speaking, enough is as good as a mall.

When clothing really *is* needed, I've got a handful of hacks to suggest. Otherwise, your dollars have better places to go than toward accessorizing. Food, shelter, utilities and getting to work (or getting to the search for work) should be the top priorities, followed closely by saving for emergencies and retirement.

Seriously: Don't shop. At all. There's no reason to go into a clothing store unless you need something. "Just looking" can quickly morph into impulse buying. So what if that so-*cuuuute* shirt from the clearance rack was only $4? If you don't need it, it's no bargain.

I've heard women justify their shopping in terms of a search for professional attire. They're "investing" in clothing because it's important to have a varied wardrobe. A couple of thoughts on that:

- Clothing is not an investment. It does not appreciate in value.
- Men who wear suits to work probably aren't stressing over whether their cufflinks, ties and shirts are varied enough.

No doubt female professionals are held to different standards in some jobs. Their attire is judged more critically than that of their male colleagues, who can get away with a few decent suits and six or seven shirts.

Be honest, though: Does anyone *really* notice what you wear to work, as long as you hit all the points of the workplace dress code? If not, think about why you feel you need to keep upgrading.

Maybe you've been listening to ads that talk about "new spring arrivals" and "updating your fall wardrobe." Or maybe shopping with girlfriends was a fun high-school outing that continued long past college because it never did you any harm.

Except that now it might. People with money issues or who are anticipating them *must* throttle back on shopping. Those of you who want to live more intentionally should also stay out of the mall, including the virtual one.

Price isn't *always* an object

The no-buy zone is harder to enforce these days thanks to the 24/7 parade of *deals! deals! deals!* Even if you don't watch TV or listen to the radio, you're likely to be pummeled by online ads or social-media shares of a friend's terrific fashion finds.

In fact, clothing has gotten so cheap that sometimes people buy because they can't think of a reason *not* to do it. Fashion and lifestyle bloggers run "haul photos" (or videos) of their most recent purchases. *These jeans were only $6! What a steal!*

But if you don't need any jeans, what's the point of buying them? Besides, unless you're in a secondhand store those $6 jeans may not be such a bargain, since inexpensively made "fast fashion" tends not to last as long. If you're on a very tight budget, put your dollars where they'll do you the most good – and that's generally not in a cheaper-than-cheap fashion retailer.

Try to keep your teenagers out of there, too, although that may be a losing battle. Your kids probably want to shop where their friends do, unless you're raising an iconoclast who rails against shallow consumerist culture or a stylista who can walk into a thrift store with $20 and come out looking like a fashion shoot.

Let them know that fast fashion probably won't last. Point out the human rights issues associated with mass production of cheap clothing overseas and the ecological fallout (disposable clothing = untold tons of junk into landfills).

And if they still want to go to The Emporium of Shoddy Churn? Let them – as long as they're shopping with their own money. They'll learn soon enough that cheaply made stuff may look bad and fit worse after a few wearings and washings. Refrain from saying "I told you so."

New, or new to you?

Those thrift shops are a great place to begin. Some of us were buying there long before Macklemore & Ryan Lewis made it hip-hop-cool. Even so, some people still think that *la segunda* is low-rent and/or that it has a funny smell.

The smell part may be true. Some of the things I get from Value Village or Goodwill do seem a bit musty, but laundering fixes that. If the fragrance is particularly dank, add a cup of vinegar to the wash cycle.

As for the low-rent aspect, I think of thrift store shopping as a treasure hunt. You might get a designer-label shirt for a couple of bucks or a good-quality wool sweater for 50 cents. On the other hand, you may get nothing. Thrift shops often arrange garments not just by size and type but also by color; if you need a white shirt with a collar for your job, you'll know pretty quickly whether it's in stock or not.

Cousin to the thrift shop is the consignment store, which offers higher-end stuff as a rule rather than as a lucky find. You'll pay more here but the pickings could be better. While shoppers do find amazing stuff at The Salvation Army or the St. Vincent de Paul, a consignment store is a good fallback if you get that new job and need decent slacks and shirts tomorrow.

Keep these tips in mind when buying at either secondhand or consignment stores:

- Try it on! One manufacturer's size 4 is another company's size 8. If there's no changing room, leave. (Or do what a friend of mine does: Wear tights and a sports bra that day so you can try on clothes without ending up on YouTube.)

- Examine garments closely for rips, stains or missing buttons. Make sure the zippers work.

- Check the return policy. You might get only a store credit, and it might be necessary to use that credit in a relatively short time.

Note: Thrift stores are also great places to find birthday and holiday presents – but only if you've budgeted for them.

New to you, part 2

Yard sales are like temporary thrift stores. For a day or so you can get some great deals on all sorts of stuff, including clothes. I've seen some gorgeous garments piled on tables and hung on fences. Watch for outerwear, too; this can be a great way to outfit your kids for the winter. (Or maybe yourself: Once I bought a name-brand parka for less than $4.)

Check newspaper ads, the "garage sales" section of Craigslist or an app like Yard-Sale Treasure Map or Garage Sales By Map. Or keep an eye out for signs in your neighborhood, which tend to come out a day or so in advance. Walk to these and you'll get some exercise while you make the most of your clothing budget.

The thrift-store shopping caveats noted above apply. So do these tips:

- Practice asking, "Is this your best price?" Also practice smiling if the sales organizer replies, "Yes, I think it's a fair deal." You don't have to buy it, but you *do* have to be polite.

- On the other hand, it doesn't hurt to look at an item for a long time as though hesitating because the seller may offer a better deal. (I've had this happen.)

- If you're buying a ton of $1 shirts and pants, ask for a discount on the lone $5 item in the bunch. *I'm getting $30 worth of stuff, so is there any chance of getting a better deal on this jacket?*

Stop back by toward the end of the sale, if you can. Pickings will be slimmer but the sellers are more likely to want to deal.

Church rummage sales can be a mixed bag but you may luck out. Multi-family sales provide the most bang for the buck, especially when they take place in the tonier parts of town. The rich *are* different – they have nicer stuff.

But even up on Snob Hill the experience is akin to that of the thrift store: You may find incredible stuff or nothing at all. The thrill of the hunt is part of the experience, but some days the hunters come home empty-handed.

New to you, part 3

When you can't afford even a yard sale, try hosting a clothing swap. Invite a few like-minded (and like-bodied) friends over and ask them to bring the sweaters they never use, the slacks they swore they'd lose five pounds to fit into and any other items they'd like to trade.

A clothes-swapping party is like a personal consignment store. The difference is that it's free.

The clothes must be in good condition and all trades must be mutually agreeable. Let it be known that you will permit no cajoling or whining, even the allegedly good-natured kind. Nobody should be bullied into trading her Nordstrom dress slacks for a "Go Mets!" T-shirt.

Make a bathroom or bedroom available for try-ons at your own private Freecycle. Participants can draw numbers to see who gets first pick, or you can just let 'em have at it. The only ironclad rule: Untraded items must leave with their owners. Otherwise you'll have a lot of extra clutter in your own space.

Depending on how much space (and patience) you have, you might encourage guests to bring books and gift items as well. The friend with a fragrance allergy who got a scented candle at the office holiday party might love the chance to trade it for someone else's art journal.

You might also ask everyone to bring a small snack to share afterward, so the event can turn into a light supper. Although you'll likely get stuck with the dishes, you may also luck out and wind up with a fridge full of leftover treats.

Note: Don't put out any items given to you by anyone who's planning to attend. No matter how hard you try to explain that you no longer wear jewelry, somebody's going to wind up with hurt feelings.

Buying retail

Although I've focused thus far on secondhand venues, I don't have anything against traditional stores. It's just that if you're on a tight budget then you need to be conscious of every dollar. Why spend more than you must?

If you can't find what you need in a non-retail setting, stores like Nordstrom Rack, Ross Dress For Less and TJ Maxx have some rock-bottom deals on decently made clothing. I paid less than $30 at Nordstrom Rack for a nice pair of black pants to wear to a divorce hearing in 2004 – and they're still my go-to slacks for a speaking engagement or a night at the opera. My daughter got

Michael Kors dress pants for $40 – a price she still grumbled about, because I raised her right. The clearance rack and end-of-season sales at other stores are also good places to look.

Unless you have mad Jedi self-control, *pay with cash*. Plastic seems to give some shoppers a feeling of invulnerability. Having to take dollars out of your wallet should make you eyeball each purchase very closely indeed.

If you're absolutely sure about your size, check out the clearance sections at online retailers. Keep in mind that if the item *doesn't* fit it needs to be returned within a certain amount of time; miss the send-back date (a real possibility if life is hectic) and you'll be stuck with something you can't wear.

Again, remember that paying with plastic could tempt you to tack on "Frozen" t-shirt for your 4-year-old: *It's only $3 and she loves that movie and it's been so long since she's had a treat...*

Except that $3 here and $3 there can torpedo a tight budget. If your daughter has enough clothes, she doesn't need it – and if you've really got $3 to spare, put it toward that emergency fund.

Garment care tips

One more suggestion: Take care of your clothing. Change into casual duds when you get home from work rather than wear better-quality stuff around the house. Definitely put on your grubs before you start dinner, lest you get tomato sauce or vinaigrette on one of your work shirts.

Treat any spots promptly. Personally I recommend Shout, which has worked miracles on my own clothes. (I'm a woman who wears her meals with pride.)

Launder your garments in cold water and hang them to dry, since the clothes dryer takes years off your duds. Certain items can be washed less often; for example, there's no need to throw jeans in the hamper after a single wearing.

Keep clothing in good repair, too. Should a seam open slightly, sew it up before the tear grows larger. Immediately replace popped-off buttons rather than setting the shirt aside to be fixed "later."

If I ran the school system I'd require that basic sewing skills be taught to all students. Being able to hem up those $1 yard-sale khakis is a great way to save money. The manager of a dry-cleaning establishment told me that minor repairs were a big part of the store's income. But why pay $5 to have a button sewn on or a torn pocket repaired when you can learn how to do it via YouTube videos? Learn a few basic stitches and save yourself some dough.

8: Staying Connected

Don't even *think* of ignoring your water or power bill. Shut-offs happen. A family I know was overwhelmed by unemployment (both adults, off and on) and did not respond to the water utility's requests for payment – or even attempt to explain what was going on with their finances. Guess what the utility did?

Nobody wants to pee in a bucket long-term. The sad part is that this didn't need to happen. According to Nolo.com, a utility company probably won't bug you if you miss one bill (that is, unless you have a history of non-payment).

Miss two or three, however, and you're likely to be threatened with a shut-off – and getting it turned back on can mean forking over a security deposit. If you can't pay the bill in the first place you sure as heck can't afford a deposit.

Don't wait for the situation to become adversarial. Start by contacting your state's public utility commission (https://www.consumeraffairs.com/links/state_pucs.html) to learn about your rights. For example, some states prohibit utility shutoffs during extreme weather. Knowing this will make the following conversation a little easier, i.e., you'll know what they *can't* do to you.

Step one: Call customer service and be honest about your situation. Be specific, too. "I got laid off two months ago and have had no luck finding work" or "My husband is undergoing cancer treatment and I've had to cut my own hours to take care of him," works a lot better than, "We're going through a rough spot financially."

Step two: Ask for help setting up a payment plan and promise to pay promptly. Be realistic about what you can afford by being specific about your financial situation. This is where that financial fire drill comes in handy: You'll already know where every dollar goes.

Here's a sample script:

- "My unemployment check is $1,200 per month.
- "Of that, $1,000 goes to rent and food.
- "That leaves $200 for everything else, including my wife's blood pressure medication and the gasoline for me to get to job interviews.
- "I'd like to pay 15 percent of that amount, or $30 per month, until I am employed once more."

The customer service worker may understand that blood cannot be wrung from this particular stone. If not? That's when you go to…

Step three: Ask to speak to a supervisor and repeat your story. Do not get angry or defensive, even if it sounds as though the supervisor is following a script ("I'm sorry, sir, but we need at least a $50 monthly payment"). Say that you'll pay extra some months if you can, but that you must take care of your family's basic needs and right now your resources are extremely limited. Make it clear that you've always paid on time in the past (you have, haven't you?) and that you will catch up sooner or later.

Finding temporary aid

Some utilities offer special rates for low-income residents. If no one mentions this, ask. When I was at my lowest point financially, I paid less for electricity than my neighbors. Once I began writing for MSN Money I started paying full freight and also contributing to a fund to help people pay off their back bills.

Two more ways to keep the lights on and the toilets flushing:

- Visit the website of the Low-Income Home Energy Assistance   Program

(https://liheapch.acf.hhs.gov/profiles/energyhelp.htm),
a federal project that helps the money-stressed heat and
cool their homes.

- Go back to 211 and ask about agencies and churches
that provide short-term utility help.

Reducing costs

Maybe you're keeping pace with the bills but wish they
weren't so high. Start frugal-hacking utility usage.

Conserve water

The savings are hard to estimate because water costs vary
widely but the following tactics will lower your utility bills.
Remember that you're paying to *dispose* of the water, too – and
when I lived in Seattle the sewerage rate was twice the cost of the
water rate.

Don't let water run while you brush your teeth. You're
wasting as much as 100 gallons per month doing this.

Turn the shower off while you wash your hair or shave your
legs.

Try a "navy shower": Get wet. Turn the water off. Soap up.
Turn the water on again and rinse.

Keep a bucket in the shower and a pitcher in the kitchen sink
for those times you're waiting for the water to get hot. Use the
saved liquid for cooking, watering plants, mopping the floor or
flushing the toilet.

Repair leaky faucets. Or get someone handy to do it for you.

Install low-flow showerheads and faucet aerators.

Mulch trees, shrubs or garden beds to slow evaporation.

Gas and electricity

Heating and air conditioning can run you a bundle, especially
if you live in an extreme climate. (I'm in Anchorage, Alaska, and

my daughter's in Phoenix – plenty of commiseration about utility bills in our family!) Here are some ways to reduce the pain:

Winterize. This helps in summer as well, i.e., it helps keep the outside heat from getting in and the (expensively) cooled air from leaking out. The utility company should have pamphlets on simple fixes you can do yourself.

Layer up. Wear a T-shirt under your blouse/shirt, and maybe top it with a sweater or sweatshirt. Long underwear in cotton, polypropylene or even silk makes an astonishing difference in the indoor chill factor. Add a pair of warm socks and you can probably drop the thermostat a few degrees.

Coddle your toes. A building contractor once told me that if your feet are warm, your head is warm. As soon as you get up (or get home from work), put on felt, fur or fuzzy bunny slippers.

Follow the warmth. Hang out in the best-insulated room vs. the lovely-but-hard-to-heat "great room" that's so popular in some home designs. If there's a door, shut it so the collective body heat will help warm the space. (Bonus: The figurative warmth of togetherness.)

Consider a space heater. Fill the most comfortable room with warmth, then shut it down and allow that togetherness concept to keep things cozy. It's essential to follow the National Fire Protection Association's recommendations (http://www.nfpa.org/safety-information/for-consumers/causes/heating/heating-safety-tips) for safe operation.

Cocoon yourself. Wrap up in a chenille throw or the crocheted afghan Grandma sent you for Christmas.

Try a rice sock. Fill a sock or cloth bag with uncooked rice and heat it in the microwave for a couple of minutes. It produces solid, delicious warmth whether placed on your lap, around your neck or at your feet. (Hint: Take one to bed with you. No more cold toes!)

Block the sun. During warm months draw shades or curtains to reduce the amount of heat that gets in.

Dress in less. Wear cotton clothing, and less of it, when it's hot.

Drink a lot. That's water, not booze. Sipping cold water helps cool you from the inside.

Use fans. The elderly, the sick and those with allergies might really *need* air conditioning. Most of us can generally get along without it for at least part of the summer. No, humidity isn't fun. Neither is having the electricity turned off due to unpaid bills.

Wait until dark. The utility company might offer a lower rate for nighttime use, so do laundry and run the dishwasher during those hours.

Hang your laundry. This cuts your electric or gas bill, and there's nothing like the smell of dried-on-the-line sheets. If you have seasonal allergies or don't have a clothesline, then use drying racks indoors. (I got mine at thrift stores and yard sales.)

Stalk those energy vampires. Unplug stuff you're not using; a power strip makes this easier. (Hint: A cellphone charger pulls current even if it's not charging anything.) Put your computer to sleep when you take a break. Save your place in a video game and power down the console rather than pause it for long periods.

Launder less. Some people insist on weekly sheet-changing or a fresh towel for every bath, but this probably isn't necessary. If you've worn a shirt only for a few hours, consider hanging it up to air and then putting it back in the closet. Jeans don't have to be washed after every wear unless you work in agriculture or the stockyards. Ultimately you need to do what works for you, but at least consider relaxing your standards; not only will you save money on utilities, your clothes and linens will last longer.

Monitor media use. Do people in your family leave TVs, computers or radios on even if they're not really paying attention?

Is anyone actually *watching* that movie in the family room or has everybody drifted away? Crack down, and mean it.

Hello, it's me

If you still have a landline, contact the phone company about minimalist service plans. One disabled woman I know paid just $10 a month for a basic connection with no long-distance service, which was all she needed. You could always pay for long-distance calls with a prepaid card, which costs as little as a few cents per minute.

Before you do this, though, contact your state's public utility commission to check out other types of assistance. One nationwide program is **Lifeline Across America** (http://www.lifelinesupport.org/ls/), which has provided free phone service for qualifying low-income householders since 1985. (No matter what you may have heard, this is *not* an "Obama Phone.") The service may be a cell phone or a special discount on a landline.

Cricket and **Republic Wireless** are lower-cost alternatives to the cellular big boys. Another company, **FreedomPop**, offers a certain amount of free service if you already own a Sprint phone; or download FreedomPop's "Free Call and Text" app to get some service for iPhones or Androids. If you've got Internet access (more on that in a minute) you can use the basic version of **Skype** for free, either voice-only or with video.

Does anything less than full-time 5G smartphone service sound like deprivation? That's understandable, since some people's smartphones are extensions of their brains. But a learned behavior can be unlearned, and until times are better you need to wean yourself off 24/7 connectivity and that $200-a-month plan.

Personally, I opted for a dumbphone: a flipper that cost less than $20 at a discount department store and is still going strong after three years. The AT&T Go Phone plan I use costs $2 a day if

I use it and nothing if I don't. (That's good for unlimited talk and data, by the way.) Since then I've rid myself of the tendency to want to call people when I'm early for an appointment or taking a walk. Happily, the result has been that I'm *living* in the quieter spots of life, rather than trying to fill them with noise.

Cutting the cord

Cable television is not a basic human right. If your finances are dicey you'll need to switch to an antenna that will get you the local channels. Hulu and/or Netflix also provide a ton of TV shows and movies, for free or fairly inexpensively. Sling TV provides ESPN and ESPN2 in its 20-channel package for about $20 per month; maybe the sports fanatic in your household is willing to use a chunk of his or her fun money for this.

A few other media options:

The public library. Get entire seasons' worth of TV shows for free. Yes, you'll have to wait for months to see what happened to the good guys (and the bad ones) on "Agents of S.H.I.E.L.D." Life will go on. In the meantime, use the library freebies to catch up on shows you always *meant* to watch. (I've still never seen "Breaking Bad." Maybe someday.)

Amazon Prime. If you were already a Prime member when your finances went south, use the heck out of the free movies and TV shows available. Just be sure to cancel the service before you're automatically billed for another year's worth. That's $99 you can use some other way.

Network websites. Some or all of your favorite shows will likely be stream-able as soon as 24 hours after airing.

For the last two options you'll need Internet access, which is now considered to be an essential utility. Some may disagree, but the fact is you can use it to apply for services and jobs, sniff out low-cost recipes other frugal hacks, and maybe even get some part-time work (more on this in Chapter 9).

If you've cut cable you've probably chopped the Internet as well, but inexpensive and even free alternatives exist.

Got a laptop? Scope out free wi-fi signals via sites like WiFi Free Spot (http://www.wififreespot.com/). This could be as simple as sitting in your car or on a public bench near a particularly strong signal.

Many libraries now offer wi-fi, and probably public computers (although their use may be limited to a couple of hours a day). You can job-hunt, catch up with friends or bring your headphones and stream the TV or movies you can no longer catch at home.

Sometimes I joke about my 25-cent office space rental, at a nearby McDonald's that offers a "senior" coffee/soft drink for a quarter. Your mileage may vary, but I've used the wi-fi for hours, sipping from that refillable cup until I turn beige. Incidentally, you may not have to be in your 60s: I first started getting this deal at age 54. In fact, the employee told me that he'd been instructed to give the discount to whoever asked for it rather than require proof of age. Just sayin'.

9: Making A Living (Or A Little Extra)

This chapter offers tips on bringing in extra income, whatever the reason:

- A current job that's not enough to pay the bills
- You're keeping the books balanced but want to get ahead
- You have a long-term goal and want to slam some serious simoleons into savings
- You got laid off

About that last: The first order of business is to find out whether you're eligible for unemployment. Learn how at the U.S. Department of Labor website, https://www.dol.gov/general/topic/unemployment-insurance.

Ideally you'll be hired next week at an even better job in your chosen field. Since we don't live in an ideal world, remember that you have to pay the bills until that dream job turns up. In other words, if your unemployment is getting close to running out – or if you didn't qualify to begin with – don't turn up your nose at a part-time gig.

Maintain an open mind about the types of work for which you'll apply. For example, if you need cash ASAP look for a day labor company in your area. You have to fork over a fee, but you'll be paid at the end of your shift. Check with temp agencies for office jobs or other short-term gigs.

Sure, it may feel odd to answer phones as a temp or build raised beds in somebody's yard. But a relatively small paycheck beats the heck out of no money at all. Think of this as a "lifeboat job," i.e., one that keeps you afloat until your real ship comes in.

Note: If the money you'd earn would be eaten up by child care and/or commuting costs, then you should keep looking. Sad to say, but sometimes it makes sense to stick with unemployment a little while longer.

The following tips apply to the unemployed, the underemployed and those who are fully employed but need (or want) to earn more.

Skilled or semi-skilled options

An obvious tactic would be to make money doing what you already do. Someone who does web design for a living could offer the same service after-hours. A waiter might look for occasional work as a banquet server, and a laid-off teacher could put himself out there as a tutor.

Speaking of teaching: If you have even *some* rapport/patience with children, consider signing up as a substitute. Some school districts will let you sub without a teaching degree, or any degree at all; in fact, some states will let you sub with just a GED.

A website called STEDI.org (http://stedi.org/subs/resources/becoming-substitute-teacher/) maintains a state-by-state list of requirements. This job will likely require a background check and a drug test, both of which take time. In other words, you won't make money tomorrow.

Helping hands

Another job that may require some certifying but always seems to have positions open is in-home care, for the elderly or those with chronic illnesses or disabilities. While some of these positions may require certified nursing assistant training, not all such gigs require super-specialized knowledge.

Some might not even require a background check if they're obtained via friend-of-a-friend referrals. For example, a relative's neighbor had a stroke and needed someone temporarily to do light housework, check her feet before helping her put on her shoes (she was also diabetic), cook a few basic items and change the catbox.

The pay was a couple of dollars more than minimum wage and the work left me feeling that I was making a difference. More to the point, I was hired immediately after speaking with the neighbor and I got paid at the end of the week.

So yes, sometimes it's not what you know but *who* you know, which is why you should put it out in the universe that you're looking for work. Tell everyone and ask those folks to pass your name along. Doing this on social media will exponentially increase your visibility; it's up to you whether it would be too embarrassing to let people know you're struggling financially. (Hint: You're probably not the only one who's in this fix.)

Here's something else that's embarrassing: Not having gas money or subway fare to get to a "real" job interview. You shouldn't lose sight of the position you'd *rather* have, but until that offer arrives then you do what you must to bring in some stopgap dollars.

Get a side hustle

Some people augment their full-time jobs with extra work, whether to build savings or to keep up with the ever-increasing cost of living. Even if you don't have a specific talent like carpentry or web design, chances are you can find something to bring in a few extra bucks.

Once I interviewed a woman who offered to walk the neighbors' kids to school along with her own. That meant she got $5 per child per day for doing something she'd be doing anyway. An at-home parent could offer school-age child care on snow days, in-service days, during winter or spring breaks, or all summer. (Think of it as "instant play date," then hope the kids all get along.)

While not all of the following ideas will work for everyone, you'll likely find at least one that resonates.

Deliver it. Newspapers. Pizzas. Packages from private carriers, which always hire during the holidays and may want someone part-time the rest of the year.

Care for cars. Offer to vacuum, wash and wax; if you're really good at this, call yourself an auto detailer and get meticulous on someone's Prius.

Care for pets. Look in on cats, fish, ferrets or whatever while their owners are on vacation. Advertise your services as a dog walker, emphasizing how nice it would be for owners will be to come home to calmer, well-exercised pooches. And speaking of jobs people don't like…

Scoop poop. Offer to clean out back yards. Fun? No. But their waste is your gain.

Be a house-sitter. That could mean staying in the place or coming by to water plants, pick up mail and make the place look lived-in.

Be a babysitter. As a midlife college student in Seattle I earned $10 or more per hour to watch kids who sometimes went to bed an hour after I arrived. It was like being paid to study.

Provide yard care. Mow lawns, trim hedges, weed the garden beds, clean leaves out of the rain gutters.

Show up. Let relatives, friends and neighbors know that you'd be glad to let a repair person in and out. Ditto signing for expected deliveries or picking up packages at the post office. That way they won't have to take half a day off from work to wait for the plumber, or worry about someone stealing those Amazon boxes off the porch.

Be a guinea pig. Not all clinical trials require you to take medications, and some of them are as simple as giving a blood sample. (Once as part of a university study I was paid $35 to fill out a form and watch an adult film made by women. I am not making that up.) I found most of my medical testing gigs through ads in student and independent newspapers, on bulletin boards at a university and, believe it or not, through Craigslist. Or just Google for opps in your area.

Fix stuff, then sell it. Good at tinkering? Keep an eye out for discarded weed-whackers and lawnmowers and such that have been discarded by Dumpsters or left on curbs. Sometimes all they need are tune-ups or new spark plugs. I once interviewed a guy who made quite a nice sideline out of flipping seemingly dead machinery.

Look for other potentially valuable discards, too. Sometimes people toss out perfectly good items because they're trading up, or because they're moving and don't want to haul everything. Sometimes these "curb mart" deals can mean big bucks. A friend's sister brought home a four-piece wicker porch set that a neighbor had set out with the trash. She dusted it, styled it with cushions and patio accessories, took a picture and put it up on her town's Facebook yard sale page.

It sold for $150 almost immediately; in fact, disappointed would-be buyers asked to be put on a waiting list in case the sale fell through. The entire process took about half an hour. Not a bad way to earn some extra cash.

While I'm not suggesting you turn your spare room into a storehouse of junk, you might find things you can clean up and sell – and again, some of this stuff doesn't even need to be cleaned, just resold. This is especially true if you live near a college or university, because students throw out a whole lot of stuff that won't fit neatly into the overhead compartment.

Clean up. Great at organizing? Let people know you'll clean out garages, basements and attics. (Hint: If they're getting rid of stuff, watch for those saleable items.)

Sell your skills

Certain specialized knowledge sets lend themselves to at-home gigs. The advantages are several: no commute, no dress code, maybe even no need to buy specialized tools or equipment if you've done this kind of work in the past.

Writing, editing, data entry, medical transcription, web design, e-book formatting, illustration and other gigs are available at sites like Freelancer.com and Upwork (formerly Elance). It's possible to get work locally by reading want ads or marketing/positioning yourself shrewdly.

Suppose you're a skilled illustrator and have helped friends through the digital publishing process (or done a book or two of your own). You could call yourself an "e-book packager" and put the word out via local writing groups.

Maybe you're organized, a fast learner and have an eye for detail. Are you in luck: A niche that's growing by leaps and bounds is the "virtual assistant," who gets people through tasks they can't/don't want to do themselves. That might consist of e-grunt work (formatting items for a deals website, say), appointment scheduling or vetting e-mails for an individual or company that gets thousands of 'em.

Then again, you might also end up doing editorial tasks. One well-known blogger of my acquaintance has a VA doing a daily "news you can use" feature for her company's website; another has the VA writing book reviews.

Note: Depending on your field, you could find the marketplace flooded with eager workers willing to do (whatever) for less. Try not to undervalue your skills, and look for employers who want good work rather than quick fixes. If you're going to spend hours on a page design or a feature article for $15 before taxes, you'd be better off working at a fast-food joint.

Sell crafts and/or belongings

An often-cited money hack is to get rid of all the extra stuff you bought when times were good. Even if you don't have pricey electronics lying around begging for a shot at eBay stardom, you might be surprised at what people want to buy.

Check the "wanted" section of Craigslist (or eBay) to get a glimpse of the sorts of things buyers are interested in obtaining. Next, go through your house from attic to basement and check garage/outbuildings. Somebody might want those swim fins, license plates, books, beer steins, Legos or bowling balls.

Some people make decent coin from Etsy, selling handcrafted or vintage items or crafts supplies. To do this you need to be consistent, since an Etsy store isn't something you can do only when you feel like it. Once I interviewed a woman who sells custom cloth handbags. She and her husband spent most of their evenings and a good chunk of their weekends cutting, sewing, embellishing and shipping their wares.

Were they thankful for the success? You bet: His company had stopped providing retirement benefits and they were anxious to set aside extra cash. But the second job was, in fact, a real job – and it was tiring. So if you start an Etsy store I wish you luck, and also suggest you figure out how you'd handle things should your wares take off.

The gig economy

Some people make decent coin with "microjobs," which are short-term or even one-time gigs you pick up from virtual employment offices like Freelancer.com, TaskRabbit and Guru. On another site, Fiverr, you put up an ad for your own products and services; the starting pay is $5 (minus the fee to Fiverr) but you can charge more if you offer extras like 24-hour turnaround. I've interviewed folks who make their entire living this way.

The variety of assignments is astonishing, from logo design to helping someone move a few boxes. You might score a gig as a virtual assistant or copywriter, or you might be asked to jailbreak an iPhone or put together IKEA furniture. If any such jobs are available in your area you could apply for as many as possible, or just use them to fill in the hours not consumed by any part-time work you've found.

Although some folks swear by Uber and other driving gigs, keep in mind that you'll be taking years off the useful life of your vehicle and that your earnings may not be vast. One former driver told The Washington Post that after taxes, gas and maintenance/repairs he was clearing about $3 per hour. Your mileage may vary, as it were, but if you're planning to try this please do some reading on the subject and go into it with your eyes open.

Incidentally, microjobs are also a good way to test the waters for a business you want to create, especially if that involves figuring out what people need done but don't have time to/don't want to do. For example, I once interviewed a college student who advertised herself as a "personal concierge service." Ultimately it turned into a full-time job doing things like grocery shopping, setting up for dinner parties and collecting dry cleaning.

Find a niche and fill it – and then profit from it. That's the American way.

Take surveys

You won't earn a living wage doing this, but if you pick your spots you'll bring in extra money and/or gift cards, and maybe even get some new products to test. I was paid to cook a taco dinner, try a new shampoo, use a new kind of mop, eat a new variety of chocolate chip cookie and join a focus group about doughnuts (earning $60 for less than three hours' worth of work).

People in certain demographics, such as "new parent" or "eats a lot of convenience food" are highly sought-after. So are men and members of minority groups.

The trick is finding the best sites, vs. the ones that pay in sweepstakes entries (seriously?) or in points that take for-*evah* to add up to anything useful.

All you need is an Internet connection and the ability to scope out the right survey venues. Some of the better sites out there are Harris Polls, ZoomPanel, Pinecone Research, Toluna and ClearVoice.

Avoid any survey sites that:

- Pay 100 points at a time – with rewards that cost tens of thousands of points apiece
- Pay in sweepstakes entries (come *on*)
- Require you to subscribe to magazines or book clubs and then take a "survey" rating the experience (these are actually affiliate marketers)

About that last: You should never have to pay to take or complete a survey. Companies are supposed to pay *you*. "Membership fee" is synonymous with "scam." Start a new e-mail address just for the surveys, and never give out bank info; you should be paid in gift cards or by check or PayPal.

Surveys aren't right for everyone. Anyone who's unemployed, at home a lot, working a late-night shift with little to do or given to lying around surfing the Internet can bring in a few (or more than a few) extra bucks. You might get sent cookies or a mop, too.

Be a snoop

Mystery shopping is not a scam – I've done it myself – but sometimes scammers promote mystery shopping lists or mystery shopping "memberships." I once got a phishing e-mail asking me to sign up as a shopper by providing my name, date of birth, Social Security number and bank account information.

Riiight.

Don't believe any of this. You can get all the info you need for free from places like Volition.com and MSPA North America (formerly the Mystery Shopping Providers Association). Another option is market research companies like ConsumerOpinionServices.com and FocusGroup.com, which seek people for product testing, screening potential advertisements, mock juries and other activities.

Secret shoppers are the eyes on the ground for a company that wants to make sure the bank teller is suggesting credit cards or the movie-theater employee is up-selling the popcorn. It can be a fun way to make a few dollars but it's likely not a good fit for those living on the margin – you're often required to pay for something upfront and be reimbursed later.

However, those who can afford the initial outlay could find that mystery shopping a fun boost to the budget. For example:

Want to take a spouse/BFF out to lunch? Look for restaurant-review mystery shopping opportunities (henceforth referred to as "shops").

Don't have a car and want to do visit a friend in the next town over? Sign up for a car-rental shop.

Do have a car? Look for an oil-change opp.

Need your eyes examined? There's a shop for that! It includes the exam and may include partial payment toward new frames.

Animal owner? Take advantage of pet-store shops. (Yep, that's a thing; one woman I know who did this was given numerous samples of high-end food items.)

Wishing you could afford something fun now and then? My daughter has gotten hotel shops that let her stay in very nice digs, use the pool and hot tub, and order room service. Abby was also paid to spend the day at a water park; on another occasion, to visit a casino (she was reimbursed for the gambling). Once she was even required to eat at Ruth's Chris; fortunately, she and her husband are very brave.

Not *all* fun and games

This does take work. You have to pay very close attention, maybe follow a script, and fill out forms carefully. Some clients call for surreptitious filming. Do any of this wrong and you may not get paid.

You'll need a PayPal account, since that's generally how shoppers are paid. Sign up with a couple of companies in your area and follow their instructions on how to look for and request jobs.

It can take time to establish yourself but as you develop a reputation for delivering reports on time and correctly supervisors might start contacting you personally, especially when other shoppers flake on them at the last minute (and you might even be offered a bonus).

One more thing: **Ignore all mystery shopping come-ons that involve cashing checks.** The premise is that you're evaluating a money-wiring services. You'll be sent a check to cash at your own bank and then asked to wire the money to the mystery shopping company. I probably don't have to tell you the ending of that story.

Rent what you own

Seems like everyone's an innkeeper these days. Airbnb, Vacation Rentals By Owner and other websites exist to hook up dollar-wise travelers with your spare room.

Inviting strangers into your home may sound scary but chances are everything will turn out just fine. If that weren't the case then all those VRBO and Airbnb folks would have given up in disgust by now. To be on the safe side, keep valuables and sensitive paperwork in a safe or a locked file cabinet (which you should be doing anyway, in case of burglary).

Hosting isn't for everyone, but it's a quick way to make hundreds or even thousands of dollars. Here's the beauty part: If you rent some or all of your primary residence for 14 days or fewer per year, you don't have to pay taxes on what you earn. (http://www.irs.gov/pub/irs-pdf/p527.pdf)

Worried about those strangers? Narrow the risk by:

- Renting through word of mouth: Let family and friends know that you're looking to host visitors occasionally. Maybe someone will be referred.

- Linking through organizations/unions/service clubs: If a Delta Sigma Theta sister or a fellow librarian comes to town for an awards banquet or conference, maybe s/he would rather stay in a home than a hotel.

- Going through your alma mater: Live near the college/university you attended? Maybe the admissions office/alumni association can put you on a lodgings list for parents touring colleges with their kids, or for graduation or homecoming.

Speaking of higher education: Consider renting your spare room to a college kid. A woman I know who lives close to a major university rented to international students once her own children left home. They were very serious and respectful of the home and of one another, she said.

Your mileage may vary, of course, so lay out your house rules ahead of time. Have the student sign a contract promising to abide by those rules.

More innkeeper tips

About those contracts: Any time you rent, you need a lease. Search online for "rental agreements" or "lease agreements" and tinker them to fit your situation. Give a copy to each renter, whether it's for Derby Weekend or the next four years of college.

Encourage long-term occupants to buy renters insurance, and talk to your own agent to see if you need to adjust your homeowners policy. In addition, have your insurance agent specifically exclude lodgers from the auto policy; that way you're protected if one of them borrows a vehicle without your permission.

For short-term rentals, offer more than just a bed and some towels. Provide freshly baked cookies in the room and access to coffee and tea, or have your guest's favorite kind of cereal handy. A list of attractions is helpful, especially if it includes shortcuts that don't involve the freeway and some tips on where the locals drink and dine.

Renting a pet?

Since parking is at a premium, consider leasing wheel space. One woman I interviewed for MSN Money rented her condo parking spot and stashed her own vehicle on the street. The monthly money was well worth the minor hassle, she said.

Someone I know in Chicago inherited a big place with a carriage-house-turned garage that had room for five vehicles. She rents four of them and turns a nice profit because secure parking is worth hundreds of dollars per month in a big city.

Finally, other people might want to rent some of your belongings. Sites like Loanables and Zilok will help you find folks willing to pay to borrow your barbecue grill, power tools, vehicle, formal wear, blender, extension ladder or whatever. One couple even rented out the family dog.

Even in the best situation – dream tenant, considerate vehicle owner – some amount of work is required when renting a room or a parking spot. For some people, the potential risks/fear factor outweigh the potential profits. But renting what's yours, whether it's a card table or the spare room, could help you eliminate debt or fund a dream.

Piecing together a living

Does all this sound complicated? It could be, especially if you wind up with a mad patchwork of part-time gigs instead of one full-time one, or trying to mesh a side hustle or two with your day job.

Maybe it won't be ideal. But if you plan carefully you'll still have parts of days available for family time and, if need be, for interviews for full-time employment.

Equally important: You'll be taking care of business. As my dad says, "That's why they call it 'work.' If it were fun, they'd call it 'fun'." The bills must be paid until times get better. Step up.

10: Entertainment On A Budget

Frugality does not mean a one-way ticket to the Land of No Fun At All. Even if times are very, very tight you can generally find diversion on the cheap.

Staying in all the time isn't optimal. Rarely seeing other people can leave you feeling glum and isolated, and maybe a little ashamed that you can no longer afford to paint the town. Even modest activities will help get you out of your own head as well your own house.

If at all possible, include "fun" as a line item in your budget. Even if it's only $5 a week (or a month), knowing that you have a few splurge bucks can boost morale. You may choose to go with mostly free stuff and let the fun fund accumulate, in order to attend one or two major events per year: a concert, play, ballgame or whatever floats your boat.

Everyone has his or her own definition of what's fun and what isn't. Pick and choose from among the following tactics to craft an affordable mix of entertainment at home and away, and for singles, couples and kids.

Getting started

In terms of free stuff, the local or regional newspaper is a great place to begin. Read it online or at the library, or look for discarded copies at a coffee shop or fast-food place. Always check it on Thursday or Friday, when arts or entertainment sections highlight local goings-on; if you're lucky, the activities calendar will have a "free events" section. If not, check all the listings for possibilities.

Read the paper during the week, too. Look for a "today in [your city]" section, where you can get clued in about lunchtime concerts, library activities, talks and the like.

Larger cities have the budget (and the audiences) for free outdoor concerts, plays and other entertainment. But even smaller communities will stage a Kite Day or a Midsummer Frolic. These will get you out of the house and socializing, and your kid may have a chance to do a craft or get his face painted for free. Have a full meal before you go, and bring some kind of snack (even if it's just peanut-butter crackers and a Thermos of lemonade) so that you and/or your kids will have something to eat later.

Yes, it might be hard to see other people gnawing on barbecued turkey legs or sucking down snow cones. But at least you'll get a day of fun – and maybe even some free stuff, since some festivals have prize drawings.

Speaking of winning: Look for trade shows in your area, such as a home and garden expo or the boat show. Some don't charge admission and most tend to be loaded with giveaways. Maybe you aren't remodeling any time soon and you certainly can't afford an RV or a boat right now. But it's an afternoon out, and some of these shows have special activities for children (who will also like going in and out of those RVs). Radio stations doing remote broadcasts from these events often give away T-shirts, CDs and other goodies, some of which make good gifts.

Even if you don't win a *FABULOUS PRIZE* you'll probably come home from the trade show with a pocket full of sweets, since most tables feature candy dishes. Some dealers also give away pencils, key chains, whistles and other items that your kids will enjoy.

And if you *do* win that gas grill or Coleman cooler? Sell it on Craigslist or give it to someone for Christmas.

Arts and entertainment

Free movies. Sign up for previews at sites such as Wild About Movies, AdvanceScreenings.com, GetScreening.com and gofobo. Or use Twitter to follow @screeningticket and @screenings. Radio stations give away preview passes. Screenings are sometimes advertised in indie newspapers. Or use points from rewards sites like Swagbucks and MyPoints (see Chapter 2) to get Regal Cinemas or Fandango gift cards. If you live near an AMC theater, save codes from Coca-Cola products and cash in for AMC tickets.

PWYC. That stands for "pay what you can," also known as "pay what you will," and it's just what it sounds like: A night out at a price you choose. Theater and comedy companies often present at least one such performance per run (or month). Do a search for opportunities in your area.

First Fridays. Maybe they call it First Thursday in your city, or Art Walk. The basic premise: All the arts venues open shows on the same evening to get maximum attention/appreciation. Going from gallery to museum to college art center makes for an inexpensive night of culture. You'll almost certainly get fed, usually cheese and fruit and wine but sometimes fancier stuff. (This is a great frugal date night.)

School days. Check out high-school concerts and theater – you might be pleasantly surprised at the quality of the performances. Some will be free.

Post-secondary school days. Live near a college or university? Watch for music, theater, lectures, symposia and art shows, some of which won't cost a dime.

Open mic. Watch for music, spoken word or performance art programs at coffeehouses and bars. Sometimes there's a cover or you might be expected to buy a cup of coffee, but that's still some pretty cheap fun. Who knows: You might hear the Next Big Thing before s/he is widely known.

Author events. Bookstores hope you'll buy a copy, of course, but it generally isn't mandatory. Listen to the author talk about writing, research and story. You might even get snacks. (Another good one for frugal date nights.)

Museums for free

Ask your local institutions about regularly scheduled free days (generally at least one per month). But that's just one of a handful of gratis culture options:

Museum Day Live! This once-a-year gift from Smithsonian magazine lets you get in free to one of more than 1,500 museums in all 50 states. You have to register in advance and then print out an e-mailed ticket. Visit www.smithsonianmag.com/museumday to find out when this year's event takes place.

Museums On Us (http://museums.bankofamerica.com). Anyone with a Bank of America bank account or a BofA or Merrill Lynch credit/debit card can get in for free on the first Saturday of the month (and Sundays in some areas). In addition to the fine arts you can get into some amazing places like the National Cowboy & Western Heritage Museum, the Country Music Hall of Fame, the Brooklyn Children's Museum, the Whitney Museum of American Art, the Shedd Aquarium and the Henry Ford Museum.

Museum reciprocity. Five organizations make it possible for you to join one institution and get free or discounted admission to numerous others. (Frugal tip: A museum membership is a good thing to ask for at Christmas or for your birthday.) Search online for the following groups:

North American Reciprocal Museum Association (https://narmassociation.org/), a hugely varied array of institutions in the United States and four other countries.

Southeastern Reciprocal Membership program (http://www.semcdirect.net/page-1241080), which includes museums in 12 states, Puerto Rico and the U.S. Virgin Islands.

The Association of Science and Technology Centers (http://www.astc.org/), with more than 600 member institutions in nearly 50 countries.

The Association of Zoos and Aquariums (https://www.aza.org/Membership/detail.aspx?id=349), offering free or discounted admission to more than 220 accredited institutions.

The Association of Children's Museums (http://www.childrensmuseums.org/childrens-museums/reciprocal-program-benefits), a network of 200 museums offering half-off general admission.

The host with the least (expense)

Depending on where you are in life and your idea of a good time, you can drum up a lot of reasons to celebrate. Be innovative about keeping costs down and you can have as many parties as you want. Some examples:

Academy Awards bash. Invite fellow film fans and serve – what else? – popcorn. Make it on top of the stove (ridiculously cheap!) and dress it up with some of the intriguing flavors suggested by the National Popcorn Board (http://recipes.popcorn.org/). Surprise them with flavors like Blazing Buffalo Ranch, Asian Popcorn Medley, Adobo and Roasted Peanut, Cajun Corn or Bombay Popcorn. Serve iced tea and lemonade and/or ask friends to bring beer and soft drinks to share.

Movie night. Pretty much the same as an Academy Awards party, but with actual films to watch. Get them from the library or meet at the home of a friend who has Netflix. Create a theme such as "Mad Max Then And Now," "Brat Pack Flashback," "Harrison

Ford Through The Ages" and "Which Was Better, The Book Or The Movie?" The binge-watching ones will take a long time, so start right after lunch on a Saturday.

Any kind of sports. A local team, your alma mater's, pro sports playoffs or the Super Bowl – some people just like to cheer and paint their faces. You can make it a potluck and start way before the game, or just provide a couple of basic snacks (like popcorn) and ask people to bring appetizers and/or beverages to share. Get corn tortillas from a bakery outlet or warehouse store, cut into strips and fry until crispy, then sprinkle with salt and set out with salsa (which you can ask someone else to bring). Buy store-brand Chex on sale and do a search for "interesting Chex mix recipes." Provide iced tea and lemonade; if some people want beer or hard stuff, let *them* bring it.

Murder mystery night. If your friends are fans of the game "Clue" and/or mystery books and TV shows, stage a role-playing game. Download free scripts at Whodunit Mysteries (http://www.whodunitmysteries.com/games.html) and Murder Mystery Parties (http://homepage.ntlworld.com/j.coutts1/main.htm). Send dossiers to the guests ahead of time so they can get into character; costumes are optional but a lot of fun.

Have a potluck. This is a great way to feed a big crowd for a small amount of money. If the first couple of events wind up being one Costco chicken, a bagged salad and six kinds of chips, consider some kind of sign-up sheet. Themes like "appetizers only," "vegan challenge" or "my favorite ethnic dish" can be fun, too.

Games night. Board games, poker, Cards Against Humanity, charades or whatever you like. Games are cheap at thrift stores (make sure no pieces are missing), and your friends may have some to share.

Book club. Make yours a safe zone: You don't have to wax poetic about symbolism and denouement, and it's also OK to say that you liked the movie more. (A little later in this chapter I'll give you numerous sources for downloading free e-books, including modern ones.)

Sleepover! Just like the fifth-grade kind, except with liquor and perspective. Invite a couple of pals to eat fun food, drink the amount that feels right, do spa stuff like manicures and facials, watch movies and, yeah, talk about romance and such. This is more likely to go over with women friends, but who knows? Some guys *do* exfoliate.

The great outdoors

Open the door. Walk outside. Amazing, isn't it? All that diversion (much of it free) without the need for a charging cord. Some suggestions:

Our national parks (https://www.nps.gov/planyourvisit/fee-free-parks.htm). Of the more than 400 sites and parks in the system, only 127 charge a fee. Even the paying ones are free at certain times.

State and regional parks. Nature trails, interactive programs, swimming and boating areas, campsites, hiking trails, Christmas tree-cutting and more can be enjoyed for free or nearly free.

Go camping. Do a search for "free camping [your area]." No tent? Maybe you can borrow one. Leave right after an early supper so you don't have to cook (although s'mores are fun if there's a firepit), and pack a small cooler with bread, hard-boiled eggs, cheese and apples for breakfast.

Go birding. It's not just the provenance of retirees, although you can certainly learn a few things from them while you're out in the field. Join in local birding walks or get a book from the library and start building that life list. It also helps to borrow binoculars if you don't own any.

For the family

These tips come in particularly handy during school breaks, when you want your kids to experience more than just hanging around the house. Many are free.

Summer movies. A handful of theater chains host second-run film children's film screenings which are either free or cost anywhere from 50 cents to $2. Among them: Cinemaworld, Bow Tie Cinemas, Harkins Theatres, Classic Cinemas, Cinemark, Marquee Cinemas, Georgia Theater Company, Carmike Cinemas, Regal Entertainment Group and Showcase Cinemas.

Free plane rides. Kids ages 8 to 17 can soar thanks to pilots with the "Young Eagles" program. The 15- to 20-minute flights are available in all 50 states and the District of Columbia. To find programs in your area, go to www.eaa.org and click on "Education and Resources."

Reading programs. Just about every public library has some kind of summer reading challenge, which may include prizes. Contact yours to find out what's going on this summer. Barnes & Noble bookstores get kids interested in reading by offering free books in exchange for a little (fun) work. Programs vary; visit the chain's website to find out how to sign up your kids.

Free bowling. All summer long your child can get two free games per day at participating bowling centers. Prepare to pay a rental fee if your kid doesn't have his or her own bowling shoes. Still: Two free games a day, *every* day if you like. Register in advance at www.kidsbowlfree.com.

Build-it workshops. All year long Lowe's and Home Depot offer free mini-seminars for those aged 5 to 12. The kids use real tools to put together things like birdhouses, planters and mail organizers, and are sent home with free project aprons and other small treats.

iMovie camp. This is a three-day program that teaches kids between the ages of 8 and 12 to make short films. Camp takes place at Apple retail stores; sign up at http://www.apple.com/retail/camp/notify.html to be notified when registration begins.

Crafts sessions. Lakeshore Learning Center, an educational supply shop, offers free Saturday programs for kids ages 3 and older. Michael's crafts stores schedule both free family craft times and Kids' Club creativity seminars (which cost $2).

LEGO fun. Kids ages 6 to 14 can participate in free "Monthly Model Mini-Build" sessions each month. Call your local LEGO store for details.

Photo safari. Leave the house with as many cameras or phones with cameras as you own. Suggest a specific topic – "Today is Take A Picture Of A Dog Day" – and see how many breeds you can capture in a couple of hours.

Take a walk. It's so easy not to use your feet these days. Pry the kids away from the TV or computer screen and set out for a stroll. Even if your children sigh and complain, stick with it; walking together can stimulate some interesting discussions.

Bike rides. Is there a bicycle trail system in your area? Use it. Or pedal around the neighborhood with your children and then come home for lemonade or iced tea (both of which taste ambrosial when you've worked up a thirst).

Hit the library. Books! Magazines! DVDs! Plus story times, maybe live entertainment and, depending on where you live, the chance to borrow everything from toys to art to fishing gear. Seriously: Libraries are treasures.

Wash the car. Squirt one another with the hose, too, to cool off and also just for the fun of it.

Family movie night. Each week a different person picks the film. No fair complaining about Junior's choice of "Despicable

Me 2," even if you've already seen it a dozen times. Make popcorn, of course, and if possible add some fun element – challenge the kids to remember a song's lyrics, or stage a trivia contest afterward with a small prize for the winner (getting to stay up half an hour later if it's a kid, getting a free pass from a particular chore if it's an adult).

Read out loud. Poems, chapter books, short stories or entire novels. A few I'd recommend: the Harry Potter books, anything by Roald Dahl, the delightfully subversive poetry of Shel Silverstein, the short stories of Ray Bradbury. (Note: Reading aloud to a partner or spouse is also great fun.)

Camp in the yard. Set up a tent out back and spend the night there. Children may find this outrageous: *We get to be outdoors in our PJs and sleep in the yard instead of our beds!* Bonus: Using a real toilet vs. trekking to an outhouse or peeing in the bushes (which your kids might want to do anyway).

The DIY drive-in. If you've got a stand-alone television vs. a wall-mounted one, set it up in your driveway and watch a free DVD from the library. Be sure to make enough popcorn for neighbor kids or even adults who stop by to see what's up and wind up staying for the double feature.

Asphalt art show. Sidewalk chalk can generally be had at the dollar store, or you might luck out and get it for less than a buck with store coupons from Jo-Ann or Michael's. Invite neighborhood kids to join your own in drawing on the street or the sidewalk.

Have a picnic. That PBJ will taste entirely different eaten on a blanket in a park or near a river, lake or ocean. Kids in particular love the novelty of eating outdoors. However, this can also be an inexpensive yet still romantic date if you invite your sweetheart to a pretty area and pack cheese, crackers and fruit plus homemade iced tea (much cheaper than wine, and you won't get kicked out of a public park for consuming it). Don't forget a vase with a flower in it, for the ambiance, and maybe some of your date's favorite music.

Millions of free e-books

A great novel, a classic whodunit, some trashy beach reading, a dense philosophical treatise – all these and others can be yours without charge. (Bonus: No danger of a late fee!) These aren't limited to really old stuff that's now in the public domain, or to creaky old chestnuts you were forced to read in high school.

From autobiography to zoology, virtual bookshelves are bursting with choices both classics and recently published. If you've got any kind of e-reader, then millions of titles are as portable as paperbacks and take up a lot less room.

Start at your public library, since so many of them lend e-books these days. Amazon and Barnes & Noble also put up daily lists of free e-books, both new titles (often self-published) titles and classics like "A Tale of Two Cities" and "Les Miserables."

Approximately one gazillion other free titles exist. Fortunately, kind and intelligent people have created aggregator sites:

Gizmo's Freeware (http://www.techsupportalert.com/free-ebooks-audio-books-read-online-download.htm): More than 900 sites, sorted by genre, plus more than 220 sources for free audio books.

Google   Play (https://play.google.com/store/books/collection/topselling_free): Not all of the more than 4 million titles here are free, but plenty of them are.

ManyBooks.net: More than 33,000 titles – filter them by genre.

(https://openlibrary.org/subjects/accessible_book): More than 1.8 million titles published between 1008 and 2016. Wow.

Project Gutenberg (http://www.gutenberg.org/): More than 50,000 books.

Full disclosure: For some, an e-reader will never replace the delight of turning a page. But even a Luddite like me has to acknowledge the wealth of choices to be found online.

Go to the fair

Not the county or state fair, which always costs a bunch. Watch for job fairs and health fairs, the former for obvious reasons and the latter because health. Wear your best bib and tucker to the job fair and bring your résumé. And yeah, if the tables have peppermints or Hershey's Kisses, grab one or two – either to keep yourself going throughout the event or to treat your kids (or your partner) later on.

Health fairs may offer free or very reduced-price testing, and usually give away stickers, snacks and door prizes. If it's getting close to December, hang on to some of these things for stocking stuffers. Take advantage of any free or affordable tests, too. True story: I once interviewed a mountain-climbing guide who was as strong as an ox and never went to the doctor. At a health fair he thought, "Oh, why not?" and got the $20 blood panel done. It turned up a serious kidney issue, and learning about it early gave him time to explore all possible treatment options.

Watch entertainment listings for open houses and rallies, too. For example, the fire station open house is always a huge hit with kids. They get to meet real live heroes and score crayons, coloring books, firefighter hats and other goodies. (Besides, who doesn't want to sit in a fire truck? I know I do.)

Even if you don't agree with everything a party has to say, stop by the Republican/Democratic/Libertarian/Whatever rally and see if there's free fun to be had. Maybe they'll rent a bouncy house for the kids, or hand out hot dogs. Here in Alaska we have the Governor's Picnic each year; free food is by definition *good* food.

Finally, visit any regional attraction if it's free. Is there a nature center with guided hikes or a historical museum with costumed tour guides who explain how people lived before the Internet and flush toilets? Maybe your city has a cheesecake company or microbrewery that offers free tours (and, one would hope, free samples). Perhaps the municipality maintains swimming at public lakes (and skating in the winter), or a free/inexpensive summer day camp. All sorts of fun might be available right under your nose. Start looking.

11: Challenge Yourself To Save

Emergencies happen, and as a nation we're not saving for them. According to the Federal Reserve, 47 percent of U.S. residents said they wouldn't be able to cover an unexpected $400 expense without borrowing money or selling something.

You need an emergency fund – and it doesn't have to be gigantic. Some PF pundits insist you need three to six months' worth of living expenses in the bank. Others say you need a year's worth.

I say, "That's a lovely dream, but some people are lucky to have *anything* in the bank. Stop making folks feel defeated before they start."

Personal finance author Liz Weston (AskLizWeston.com) suggests that even a $500 cash cushion can cover quite a few problems. In a column on the NerdWallet website, she cited an Urban Institute study that showed savings between $250 and $749 can make a big difference for lower-income households.

Families who saved were:

- 24 percent less likely to miss a utility payment
- 28 percent less likely to miss a housing payment
- 78 percent less likely to be evicted

Thus you need to get serious about saving an emergency fund, even if you think you can't. *Especially* if you think you can't.

Sometimes it's true that it takes every dime you earn just to make bank and put basic food on the table. (Been there. It's stomach-shredding.) However, a little creativity could help you shave off a few dollars here and there for an emergency fund.

One reader called it an "Oh S--t! Fund." I understand why. When things go sideways in an already-straitened life, you just want to howl at the unfairness of it all. Even a small EF will make a difference: It may not fix everything that's wrong but it at least cuts down on the amount you have to borrow or finance.

You really *can* save

For example, suppose that bald-as-an-inner-tube tire finally dies. You have no credit/your card is maxed out. No family or friends nearby/they're as hard-up as you are. If you had put even $5 per month into an EF for the past year, you'd have enough to pay for a basic all-season, on-sale wheel. But you didn't.

What's next, then: Lose your job because you can't drive to work? Or make the damned-if-you-do, doubled-damned-if-you-don't walk to the payday loan place?

Broke people *can* save. It may take longer and it may hurt a bit. You know what else hurts? Renewing payday loans over and over because you have no recourse.

Take a tip from the title of this chapter and make saving your EF a challenge – a *fun* challenge. Set a smallish goal ("By the end of the month I will have at least $5 set aside") and set out to see how much more than $5 you can squirrel away. Get your family or roommates involved, too; nothing like a little friendly competition to rev your savings engine.

Not all the following tips will work for everyone. But at least *some* of them should get you going toward a fully funded EF, even if you literally have to nickel-and-dime your way there.

Bank on it

Automate funds. Set up a small withdrawal from each paycheck (start with at least $5), on the theory that if you don't see it, you won't miss it. That may not always be the case, but tell the truth: Haven't you ever looked at your (small) positive checking-account balance on the night before payday and decided to split a pizza with your roommate? Sure, you should allow yourself a treat now and then – but get that EF up to at least $500 and *then* indulge in celebratory pepperoni.

Save your raise. If you're lucky enough to get one, that is. Figure out what it will amount to after taxes and make that the amount of your automated withdrawal.

Bank that bonus. If you got one of those then you're a *really* lucky dog; I know only one person whose boss consistently awards these. Spend 10 percent of the amount on something you truly want/need, and put the rest into the EF. Seeing that big bump in the account should make you feel all warm and fuzzy.

Tuck away reimbursements. Got a flexible spending account, or do you get paid for work-related expenses? Try to put even 5 to 10 percent of each payment into the EF.

Save your savings. Any time you use a coupon or get a discount due to a customer loyalty card, salt away the amount of the price break. Check the bottom of your supermarket receipt for "you saved X dollars today" info. Another form of this is to…

Front-load a discount. Instead of using cash, credit or debit, pay for regularly purchased items with discounted gift cards bought on the secondary market. For example, buying a $50 Walgreens card for $44 would mean $6 for the EF. (See Chapter 2 for the ins and outs of discounted gift cards.)

Keep the Change. This Bank of America feature rounds debit-card purchases up to the next dollar, then transfers the difference into savings. Paying $25.16 at the gas pump means your EF grows by 84 cents.

Save As You Go. Sign up for this and Wells Fargo will transfer $1 from checking to savings every time you pay with your debit card, use online bill-pay or have an automatic payment deducted from checking. That didn't hurt (much), did it?

Digit. I use this personal finance app myself and like it a lot, considering it my "invisible savings." After figuring out how you earn and spend your money, Digit decides how much you can afford to spare and then sends small deposits to an online bank account a few times per week. (If you want to join, please consider using my referral link, https://digit.co/r/bydFD.)

Challenge accepted!

Frugalists just *love* a challenge, and some of these savings hacks are pretty painless even when times are tight.

The pantry challenge. Instead of joining your roomie in that pizza delivery, go prospecting in the cupboards and fridge (even if it ends up being a weird dinner like ramen, green beans and raisins). Estimate what your share of the Domino's order would have been and shoot it over to the EF. Allow yourself to feel smug, especially since you also cleared out food before it had the chance to get too old to eat.

Calendar challenge. The first week of January, bank $52; the second week, set aside $51. Keep at it and at the end of the year you'll have banked $1,378.

Weekly challenge. The first week of each month, put $1 in the jar. The second week, it's $2. You'll bank $10 to $15 per month this way.

Spare-change challenge. One of the oldest tricks in the savings book: Dump most or all of the coins from your pocket/wallet into a jar. Wrap and bank the specie every couple of months. If your bank won't accept rolled coins, well, fie on that institution! The supermarket or convenience store might want some of the change (these places go through a lot of it), or you can just use it for small purchases like a loaf of bread or a hand of bananas. Counting out $2 in quarters and dimes isn't a big deal, especially if you shop during off-hours. Finally, some people swear by those Coinstar counting machines, which charge you a fee unless you take the total in the form of a gift card; just make sure it's a retailer you were going to use anyway.

Dollar-bill challenge. This is the spare change challenge's richer cousin: Take all the ones out of your wallet at night and stuff 'em in a different jar. Or go crazy and make it a $5 bill challenge.

Found-coin challenge. Hey, somebody left a quarter in the vending machine! Or maybe it's a dropped dime at the checkout counter, a nickel on the sidewalk or a few pennies that fell through that Coinstar machine (always an excellent place to look). Money is everywhere if you don't mind picking it up. Add it to the spare-change challenge jar or start a new one.

Random number challenge. Choose a number (kids like to do this), and every night check the serial numbers of the bills in your wallet. Any that end in that number means that the bill goes into the fund.

Dare-you challenge. If you've got a relative or friend who also needs to save, suggest this: "I dare you to try and save more than me in the next three months. If I win, you have to detail my car/take me to lunch/scoop the back yard." Anyone with an ounce of competitive spirit will want to play – and no matter who ends up with more cash, you both win.

Cashing in

Recycle. If you're lucky enough to live in a place where cans and plastic bottles bring you a nickel or dime apiece, start collecting. You could pick them up on walks, ask relatives to save them for you or maybe even bring them home from the workplace lunchroom. Some places without deposit laws still let you recycle aluminum by the pound. You'll need storage space, of course, and you should also figure out whether it's worth it. (Hint: Driving 17 miles round-trip to recycle $2.29 worth of aluminum is not a smart use of your time. Or your car.)

Incentivized savings. Occasionally banks will offer a cash stimulus to get people to open accounts. Let the account be your EF, and add the incentive to it.

Join Swagbucks. What makes this rewards program different from the others is that it includes PayPal as an option. For as few as 2,200 points you can get $25 in cold, hard cash. All you need for a PayPal account is a bank or credit union account to which to link it. (See Chapter 2 for the specifics.)

Stash your rewards. Got a rewards credit card? If not, try to trade in your vanilla card for one that provides benefits, and send the cash-back amount to your EF. (See Chapter 2 for links to sites that review the best rewards credit cards.)

Look for a second job

This isn't always as easy as it sounds, especially in areas where it's hard to get a *first* job, let alone a second one. It can also be tough to work extra hours when illness or disability (your own or a family member's) presents extra challenges to your days.

However, it's also true that money-earning options you could never imagine are out there. See the "Get A Side Hustle" section of Chapter 9 for specific tips.

Adjust your habits

Quit it! It's hard to stop smoking or eating junk food, or whatever your habitual weakness happens to be. Be conscious of what you're spending and reduce it slooooowly. Calculate what you've saved each week and send those dollars to safety. Bonus: Your health should improve once you stop with the coffin nails and the greasy treats.

Rework other habits. Suppose you and a pal meet for coffee every Saturday, or that you hit blockbuster movies on opening night. A couple of times a month, replace that coffee date with a leisurely, chatty walk. Get in the habit of going to the first show on Saturday, which is much cheaper than a nighttime ticket. When you modify a habit, figure out your savings and put them in the fund.

Bring it from home. Packing your lunch can mean huge savings but think about snack habits, too. If you hit the soft-drink or candy machines once or twice a week, you're probably dropping $20 a month. Watch for loss-leader sodas and snacks and keep them in your bag/desk/locker, then send a couple of bucks a week to the EF.

Swear by it. Ever heard of the "swear jar," wherein you place a quarter every time you drop an F-bomb? Give it a try, especially if you have kids (who *love* to call you out on it) or you want to present a more professional image at work.

Reward yourself. This is the opposite of the swear jar. Say you packed a PBJ today instead of hitting the Value Menu. Good for you! Now put a dollar (or more) in the Jar of Virtue.

Money mind game

Name your dollars. My financial institution lets me assign names to sub-accounts. I've got two named for my great-nephews' college funds and a third called "Cash For New Car." Each time you send that $5 (or whatever) a week to an account named "Family Protection" or "No More Debt," you'll be reminded why you save.

It's a bill, so pay it. Free budgeting sites like Mint.com and PowerWallet have "bill reminder" features. Set up "emergency fund" as a bill, even if it's just for $5 a month. This can make it easier to factor savings into the monthly budget.

Be symbolic. Your tween will graduate high school in 2024? Save $26 (2 + 0 + 24) per month, or every other week if you can swing it. The better-equipped you are to weather financial storms the more likely it is you'll be able to help her in small ways (e.g., driving her up to the university) or big ones (letting her live at home rent-free if she attends a local college). Don't have kids? Try something like this: *I hit retirement age in 28 years, so I'll start setting aside $28 per month for emergencies.*

Remember your goal. Get a picture of something that matters to you and rubber-band it to your credit/debit card. Seeing your fiancé or your newborn might remind you *why* need to be smarter about money, and keep you from tossing a package of Slim Jims into your grocery cart while you wait in line. Or tape a Post-It note to the card – the words "emergency fund" or a more specific message like "Baby due Aug. 19" will give you a frugal goose.

Remember your goal, Part 2. Change your debit-card PIN to a date with serious resonance. It could be "0819" for the baby's due date or "2024" for your daughter's high-school graduation year. Typing in those numbers might help you talk yourself down from getting that extra $20 in walking-around money or from throwing those Slim Jims into the cart. (Frugal tip: You can ask the clerk to remove the snack from your order, and if you rethink that $20 you could put it into an envelope and deposit it back into the account.)

Laundering funds. Each time we do a load of wash at our house, $2 goes into a jar. Although we call it the "New Washing Machine Fund," it actually got used when we replaced the 30-year-old stove. Yours, of course, will go into the EF.

Save it forward. You finally paid off your (new-to-you) car. Woo hoo! Keep making the payment, though, by transferring that amount into savings each month. Can't manage that? Try to save at least half.

Round it up. Any time you use a debit card (or write a check, if you still do that), record it (assuming you still do that) as the next dollar up. For example, a $22.52 grocery trip becomes $23 in the register. At the end of the month, add up the differences and send them to the fund.

Steal from yourself. Suppose there's $37 left in checking the day before payday. Send $7 (or $17) of it to your EF.

Save money, save your finances

After you've tried one or more of these tactics you should take a minute to congratulate yourself. Saving can be very, very tough if yours is one of those households that barely keeps the books balanced. Finding "extra" money can feel laborious and taking that money away from your tighter-than-tight budget may seem downright punitive.

Again: Been there. It hurts. I did our laundry on a scrub-board and dried it on a rack because I couldn't spare the quarters for the laundromat. You know why I couldn't? Because:

- I was a single mom with no child support and a "permanent part-time" position with varying hours, and
- Every week I had the employee credit union take a chunk of my salary right off the top.

Yes, even though I was poorer than a church mouse I had a small emergency fund. When the baby got outgrew her shoes or got sick and needed a prescription, the money was there to pay for it. This was way back in the NoPlasticScene Era. At that time credit cards were just beginning to become commonplace but there was no way in hell a company would give credit to struggling-single-mom-me.

Would I have preferred to hire a babysitter and go to a movie now and then rather than set money aside each week? Or maybe to eat something other than bean soup, spaghetti, chili and oatmeal? You bet. But I knew if something went wrong it would be up to me to cover the cost. So I saved.

I urge you to do the same. Yes, sometimes it will feel like punishment. But that EF will feel like a blessing the next time life plants a surprise in your path.

12: What About The Children?

This section has a dual focus: How to help kids understand the way money works in your household, and how to meet your child's basic needs (plus some of the frills) affordably.

The first will take more than one explanation. No matter how smart you think your kids are, they probably won't truly comprehend personal finance right off the bat. (Heck, a lot of *adults* still don't get it.) What the typical kid knows about money is that it's something grownups use to buy cool stuff.

Plenty of families still consider money a taboo subject, and don't talk about things like mortgages, income tax, emergency funds and retirement savings in any substantive way. (Complaining about the size of your take-home or your tax burden doesn't count.) Thus Junior and Sister probably don't completely comprehend how much work goes into getting that salary, let alone how much of what you earn isn't really yours.

I once read about a couple who, tired of their children's lamentations and accusations, decided to show the kids how much money they made. The man and woman cashed their paychecks instead of depositing them and deposited the lucre on a dining table. Their children's eyes popped: *Wow, we're rich!*

And they weren't actually doing too badly, until Mom and Dad started creating neat little piles of obligation. This much for insurance, that much for utilities, a great big chunk for the mortgage. The monthly orthodontist payment, the grocery bill, gas allowance for two cars, and so on. What was left wasn't much, and they had to live on it all month.

Not that the kids suddenly felt A-OK about not having the things they thought they deserved. However, they at least understood (in the abstract, anyway) why they weren't getting them.

Walking your talk

You don't have to bring home your paycheck in cash to make the point. Personally, I'd suggest ongoing education in the form of your modeling savvy consumer behaviors. When you cook most (or all) meals at home, pack a lunch, mow your own lawn, comparison-shop for the best price, or get and give items via Freecycle, you're teaching kids how to be capable citizens.

Talk about your financial values, too. For example, you might:

- Explain that you buy well-made items that last vs. cheap stuff because you'd rather buy it right than buy it twice, and because it means fewer items sent to the landfill.

- Emphasize that a debt-free life is much better than worrying about how you'll pay your bills, "so we're not going to use a credit card to buy you more toys – but put that Legos set on your wish list and maybe you'll get it for Christmas."

- Discuss how satisfying a certain amount of DIY can be – repairing a porch railing, say, or growing a tomato that actually *tastes* like a tomato.

What you don't want to do is scare your children. If times are tight right now due to illness or un- or underemployment, be careful about how you frame money issues. Rather than say "We can't afford that," use the expression, "That's not in the budget right now." If they ask what a budget is, tell them it's "a spending plan to make sure our money gets used the smartest possible ways."

The way you spend is a reflection of your values and goals. To use the example above, you won't charge up a pallet o' Legos because you don't believe in accruing debt.

When things are *very* tight

Suppose your household is feeling more than just a little pinch. Perhaps unemployment, illness or some other issue has caused some serious cash-flow problems. What then?

Use every possible resource to make the best life you can, even if that means making some tough short-term decisions. For example, you might have to get rid of a car, or move to a cheaper neighborhood/bunk with your folks for a while. Sound grim? Then imagine how your money woes might feel to your kids, who aren't getting the entire picture but rather barely overhearing (and maybe misinterpreting) discussions about available cash.

No matter what upheavals are taking place in your personal life, strive to model a reasonably calm and ultimately optimistic attitude for your children. If you need to vent or even cry, do it in private or in the company of other adults. Stay as calm as you can when talking with your children.

Acknowledge the elephant in the room but reassure them that life will go on. Sample script: *We're going through some challenging times right now. Things may look different for a while and we may have to make changes we wouldn't have chosen, but we WILL get through this.*

Making tough choices

Some of those changes could involve input from the kids themselves. A child who's involved in a lot of sports or extracurriculars could be required to choose just one or two of those things, or maybe none of them. Will that be easy? No. Might it be necessary? Yes.

It helps if you've already taught them the difference between "wants" and "needs." Know going in that this will require a few iterations, or possibly a few hundred. To a child whose classmates have multiple e-gadgets, not being able to have even *one* will feel like penury. A teen whose peers got cars for their 16th birthdays may literally feel left behind. And a backyard birthday party with cake and games could feel like a terrible comedown, especially if you live in an area where birthdays are like mini-coronations.

Even if your offspring are good kids they might still complain, whine or accuse you of not understanding. *My smartphone is so old it's embarrassing! Jason's parents took him to Disney World on spring break. Emma's prom dress cost $500 and her parents rented a hotel room for the night.*

Don't take it personally. Kids are by definition self-centered, i.e., everything is about them and how it affects their place in the world. Hear them out, but stick to your guns: *All our basic needs will be met. However, the current budget does not have room for EVERYTHING we want. Let's brainstorm some ways for you to pay for some of the extras (e.g., babysitting or recycling cans).*

You might feel that it's your job to give them everything their friends have. It isn't! Please don't release an Entitlement Monster on an unsuspecting world. Your children need food, shelter and clothing. Anything else is a frill. Besides, if they don't learn money management skills at home you're setting them up for years of PF foulups once they're on their own.

Don't beat yourself up if you can no longer buy a lot of the extras. Focus on meeting all of their needs and at least a few of their wants.

Making the basics affordable

Loads of budget-stretching hacks can be found in Chapter 2 and Chapter 3. The further your money goes, the easier it is to meet your family's needs. Check out the following tips as well.

Diapers

The bottom line, as it were, is that nappies aren't cheap. Back when the earth was still cooling I used cloth diapers on my baby; although there was a bit of an ick factor they really were pretty manageable. Infants are always doing something damp and disgusting anyway, so I just rolled with it. Besides, as a broke single mom I really couldn't afford to do it any other way.

Cloth is now chic again, and the new paradigm (wipes, prefolds, covers with Velcro) makes the diapering a lot easier. Some paint it as an environmental choice; others, I think, can't wrap their heads around the idea of paying up to $2,500 for disposables from birth through toilet training. A blogger named Kerry Taylor (Squawkfox.com) ran the numbers for cloth diapers and found it cost just under $550 for everything, including laundering (and factoring in the resale value of the nappies and covers).

About that resale value: Before you spend a ton on new diapers, look for deals on Craigslist or parenting boards, or put it out in the universe that you're in the market for affordable butt-covers. Someone might just have finished toilet training and be looking to sell. You might even luck out and have some given to you by a friend or relative who knows times are tough right now.

Fact is, some people just are Not. Going. For. Cloth. Ever. Ever. Ever. You need to do what works for you, keeping these tips in mind:

Ask for what you need. If people want to know what kind of baby gifts you want, mention diapers. Often. Just make sure they're not all "newborn" size, because baby will grow out of them fairly quickly.

The no-diaper movement. Some parents swear by "elimination communication." A site called DiaperFreeBaby.org can help you learn more. If it works even part of the time that's some decent savings.

Diaper services. Your waste is their gain. Give it a try for the first month or two; if you hate it, you can opt back in for disposables.

Warehouse stores. They have consistently decent prices and sometimes offer coupons. One warehouse store, BJ's Wholesale Club, accepts manufacturer's coupons.

Amazon Family. Get a 20 percent discount when you set up regular diaper deliveries. The first three months are free; if you don't cancel after that you'll be charged for a year's worth of Amazon Prime (same benefits).

Diapers.com. This site provides good prices, coupons and free delivery – and doesn't charge a membership fee. If you shop this way, be sure to access Diapers.com through a cash-back shopping site for rebates of 3 to 4 percent per order.

Target. The store's "club packs" are brand-name nappies sold in large quantities. Stack coupons and sale prices (and maybe the 5 percent daily discount for having the Target credit card) and you could wind up beating Amazon Mom and the warehouses, according to Cassie Michael of TheThriftyCouple.com.

Join rewards programs. Some of the big brands have "baby clubs" with coupons for members. Programs like "Gifts To Grow" let you exchange points for toys and other items (one woman I interviewed bought holiday gifts this way). If you're buying from a drugstore, make sure you have a store rewards card.

Cash in rewards. Points from programs like MyPoints, Bing and Swagbucks can be traded in for gift cards, including Amazon, Target and Walgreens.

Stock up. When you find a really good price, buy as many as you have room for/can afford. Tape the sales receipt to one of the boxes, just in case your baby outgrows the size before you can use them all. (Tip: The manufacturer's suggested weights aren't necessarily accurate. Don't move your kid up a size unless the diapers no longer fit.)

Pay with a discounted gift card. Save up to 10 percent or even more on cards for Walgreens, CVS, Target and Rite Aid. (See Chapter 3 for more information.)

Clearance racks. Manufacturers actually change diaper styles, and discontinued designs will be remaindered.

Clothing and equipment

Any relatives, friends or co-workers have children? Make it known that you will happily accept outgrown duds, equipment* and playthings. As a broke single mom I was blessed to receive (and later pass along) a fair amount of stuff.

You could also formalize the arrangement by creating a clothing swap (see Chapter 7) through a parent group, place of worship, child care center or just your circle of friends. This might work best for younger kids, of course, lest a 9-year-old blurt out, "Hey, Braden is wearing my brother's old shirt!" during recess.

Speaking of new-to-you: My niece dresses her kids in designer duds that cost a teeny-tiny fraction of the original price tag. That's because she hits thrift stores and yard sales with a keen appreciation for quality (and a critical eye for spots and other damage). Not all thrift stores and yard sales are the same, of course; those lucky enough to live in large metro areas and/or near richer neighborhoods will have more options.

You won't know unless you go, so get in the habit of popping in regularly at any thrift shop you drive by or can walk to as part of an exercise regimen. You might find the toddler snowsuit of your dreams one day and then nothing at all for the next few visits. It's a total crapshoot although, as noted earlier, I prefer to think of it as a treasure hunt.

Yard sales are potential gold mines, both for clothing and other needful things. My niece likes to visit the community-wide yard sale in one of her city's tonier neighborhoods. But I've found great children's items in humbler districts, too.

A couple of secondhand strategies:

- Look for "multi-family" or "community sale" ads.

- Squirrel away that Disney DVD or beautiful children's book for your preschooler's next birthday. Or for Christmas, as part of the minimalist four-gift credo: "Something you want, something you need, something to wear, something to read.")

- Shop for others. That obviously unworn onesie from Goodwill or the church rummage sale can be a shower gift for your pregnant sister-in-law. Once I saw a spotless, adorable, 100% organic cotton bib at a yard sale for a quarter; the original price was $18. No one has to know how much you paid.

Why pay more?

Which brings me to a depressing but real fact of life: Some people consider thrift shops/yard sales to be déclassé and maybe even a little disgusting.

Thus you need to know your audience before you burble on about the *great* deal you got on those Osh Kosh B'Gosh overalls. At a family barbecue a friend of mine was complimented on how neatly turned out her kids were, and asked where the clothing had been purchased. My friend said, "Aren't they great? I got them at Goodwill."

The other woman's face did that freeze/sneer/*eeewww* thing, and she said, out loud, "Oh, I could never wear clothes other people have worn. I'd never make my kids wear them, either."

Well. Suddenly my friend felt very bad about her kiddie couture choice. Yet it's a choice she had to make because her family was getting by on a fairly lean budget.

You can bet that if parents have something against secondhand chic they'll pass that attitude along to their children. Thus you might want to tell your own kids not to mention where Mom and Dad like to shop. They might be puzzled: Why would people *want* to pay more for the same stuff?

Answer: It's complicated.

On the bright side, once your kids hit their teens they might start hanging around with the high-schoolers who think thrift shopping is retro-cool. Until then, they'd probably better keep mum about their retailers of choice.

*Back in the day it was common for cribs and car seats to be passed down. Be very, *very* careful about this practice, as some of these items may have been the subjects of safety recalls. Suppose your BFF bought the best crib and/or car seat two years ago and is promising it to you once her child graduates to a big-girl bed/booster seat. Do a discreet online search to be sure the item is up to current standards.

If so, congratulations: You just saved a ton of money. And if not? Well, for heaven's sake, tell your friend so she can take action.

An all-around workaround

Here's a character-building way to afford the extras: Let someone else pay for them. If relatives or friends want to give your kids birthday or holiday gifts, see if they'd be willing to cover sports fees or a couple of months' worth of dance lessons vs. buying games or toys.

How does someone else footing the bill encourage character development? It teaches a child to prioritize, e.g., "Instead of a handful of small/medium Christmas gifts from my grandparents I'll get to go back to theater camp – *seven months from now.* Argh! But I really want this so I'm going to do it."

Your kid will also learn how to get imaginative if he wants something he can't afford right now. And that's what my dad would call "a useful life skill."

Teacher gifts, extracurriculars and other cash grabs

It's not cheap to outfit your child for a school year, even if you use those frugal clothing hacks. Maybe your kid needs to supply her own violin for music instruction and the chance to play in the holiday concert. That intramural sports opp you thought would get your video-obsessed tween up and moving will cost you for running shoes or soccer cleats. You'll also likely be tagged for field trips, fundraising sales (wrapping paper, cookie dough and the like), class photos, school auctions and gifts for the teacher.

Make "school stuff" a line item in your budget, so your kid won't be the one who has to stay behind while classmates go to the museum or the theater. However, you don't have to say "yes" to everything that's asked of you. Take a hard look at your financial reality and then do the following:

Set limits. Decide how much money you can devote to school-related stuff. If times are tough, carve a few dollars from other parts of the budget. Suppose you and your spouse/partner allow yourselves $20 a month for fun or discretionary purchases. Would you be willing to donate $5 per month toward extras for your kid? Or perhaps you could declare Meatless Mondays and Four-Gift Christmas, the better to divert more funds toward school activities you think are really worthwhile. See Chapter 11 for tactics that will help you set aside a few dollars.

Prioritize. Go for maximum impact as well as affordability. If the school is selling wrapping paper, forget it – the stuff is wildly overpriced. But if the fundraiser is for take-and-bake pizzas then go for it; designate a couple of bucks from the "groceries" portion of the budget if necessary. (Friends and family might be willing to buy in as well if the item is anything close to worth its real price.) Similarly, if the school is sponsoring a fall festival then take the whole family and consider it fairly cheap entertainment.

Compromise. If you can't afford the cookie dough or wrapping paper but could shake loose $5, give the money directly to the PTA or the class-trip fund.

Volunteer. Even if you can't afford to buy overpriced band candy, you can still help the school. Work in the classroom, offer to help out at festivals or book sales, run errands for the teacher.

Think "cheap or free." Use points from Swagbucks and other rewards programs to buy gift cards to cover necessities. Perhaps the music teacher could find a loaner violin. Some of the stuff your kid needs (Scout gear, musical instruments) might be available through word of mouth, The Freecycle Network or the "free" section of Craigslist. Stores like Play It Again Sports offer discounts on equipment that still has a lot of wear in it.

Say "no." Consider letting your child be part of *one* fundraiser per season/per year, which limits how often friends and family will be asked to contribute. (It also saves you the stress of having to say "can't afford it, sorry.") This could force kids to make some tough choices – *classroom, Scouts or team?* – but life is all about choices.

And if any adult gives your child a hard time about this, push back politely but firmly: "My kids can't do multiple fundraisers because we don't want to keep dunning our relatives and friends." Sure, saying this may be a little embarrassing. Say it anyway, and don't let anybody second-guess your personal choices. Do what's best for your family and your finances.

An apple for the teacher?

Finally, a word about presents. Two words, actually: *not required*. And I say this even though my dad was a teacher and my sister and niece are both teachers. Naturally it's lovely to get a gift during the holidays or at the end of the school year, but It. Is. Completely. Voluntary.

Your student may feel the pressure to give. You might, also. If the budget really won't allow it, work with your child to write a letter thanking the teacher for everything s/he has done during the year. Be as specific as possible, e.g.:

- "I had trouble with reading but you believed in me. Now I go to the library every Saturday."
- "Every day I am excited to go to school."
- And maybe even the biggie: "I want to be a teacher when I grow up."

And if you *can* afford a little something? Try to suss out what the teacher could use for the classroom, such as books, magazines or art supplies (bought through cash-back sites and/or with discounted gift cards, of course). For a teacher who loves coffee or tea, even a $10 Starbucks card will be a day-brightener. Homemade treats are a good bet, unless you know that a batch of freshly made peanut brittle would sabotage her ultramarathon training.

Know this, however: No educator needs another coffee mug or "No. 1 Teacher!" plaque. Trust me.

Afterword

My sister sometimes talks about "making a decision for happiness." That doesn't mean simply deciding to be happy, however. To get there you must deal with existing challenges and also be both resourceful and flexible should any new issues crop up. (Hint: They will.)

If you're reading this you've probably had a rough year (possibly a rough run of years) or can see hard times coming. That, or you're one of those folks determined to live well on less money in order to reach a specific goal.

For all three groups I have one piece of advice: **Focus on your dream, but know it won't happen simply because you're wishing really hard.** Faith is great, but it's not enough. You've got to walk – and work! – toward change.

Set both short- and long-term goals, and use the tactics in this book to make them happen. In a perfect world your financial progress would be both immediate and meteoric. What's more realistic is to aim for slow and steady improvement, so you won't burn out.

I would love to hear from you about how this book helped – and what you'd like to see in a second book. Yes, I'm planning a sequel and I've already got a bunch of topics sketched out. Among them: travel, education (your own or someone else's), insurance, how to afford special occasions, celebrating the holidays and ways to save money on pet care.

To make sure that I'm covering what people need to know, I'd welcome feedback. Write to me at *SmartSpending@live.com.*

For additional tips on frugal living and money hackery, I recommend the following sites:

AskLizWeston.com. She's the author of a bunch of personal finance books and as her website name suggests, you can ask her anything.

BeverlyHarzog.com. A credit expert with no affiliate links to credit cards (i.e., not a hint of conflict of interest), she loves to answer reader questions.

Clark.com. How far will consumer advocate Clark Howard go to save you a buck? Pretty darned far – and he makes it so easy you'll go right along with him.

The Dollar Stretcher (http://www.stretcher.com/). Gary Foreman has been blogging about bucks since 1996. If you need an answer, he's probably got it.

EverydayCheapskate.com. The queen mother of frugality, Mary Hunt has been writing about this stuff for three decades and is the author of several dozen books. Tons o' tips here.

GerriDetweiler.com. Another credit expert who gives the straight scoop, and who has written a terrific resource called *Debt Collection Answers: How to Use Debt Collection Laws to Protect Your Rights*. You can download it absolutely free by looking under "credit resources" on her site.

IPickUpPennies.net. This is my daughter's site, the home of "imperfect frugality" – that is, an acknowledgment that not all frugal tips work for all people. Due to disability and chronic illness she's had to learn to play to her strengths and compensate for her weaknesses. In fact, she recently wrote a book called *Frugality For Depressives: Money-Saving Tactics For Those Who Find Life A Little Harder*, which is available on Amazon or through her website.

MoneyTalksNews.com. A huge array of personal finance topics and videos.

MyFrugalHome.com. The ever-resourceful Erin Huffstetler is the About.com frugal living expert and she really knows her stuff.

NerdWallet.com. Well-researched articles on just about any topic you could imagine, and tools to help you get the best deals on financial products.

PlantingMoneySeeds.com. At times it seems that Miranda Marquit has written for every personal finance blog in existence, yet somehow she finds time to write for her own site as well. She's also one-half of the Adulting.tv site, which produces podcasts and videos on questions relevant to young adults.

WiseBread.com. This long-established blog is another great source of articles on just about every money/life issue.

And, of course, my own website, **DonnaFreedman.com**, where I write about money and midlife (and whatever else comes up). Hope to see you there.

About the author

Donna Freedman has been a college dropout, a single mom, a newspaper reporter in Chicago and Alaska, and a midlife university student. She has also picked tomatoes, worked on a chicken farm, managed an apartment building, inspected and packed bottles in a glass factory, babysat, cleaned houses, mystery-shopped, participated in medical studies, set type, and sold doughnuts, movie tickets, fresh Jersey produce and, when things got bad, her own blood.

During a protracted midlife divorce she went back to school and helped support a disabled adult daughter by working a handful of part-time jobs. Her survival skills so impressed an MSN Money editor that he hired her to create the Smart Spending blog and later her own column, Living With Less. Since then she has written for numerous other online publications, including Vox Media, NerdWallet, Get Rich Slowly, Daily Worth, Experian, Money Talks News, GO Banking Rates, the Experian blog, Women & Co. (CitiBank) and Wise Bread.

Donna has also written for numerous magazines and newspapers. Her work has won awards from the Society of Professional Journalists, the Women's Sports Foundation, the National College of Allergy, Asthma & Immunology, the Association for Women in Communications, the Society of American Travel Writers, the Plutus Foundation and the Alaska Press Club.

She created the Write A Blog People Will Read online course (WriteABlogPeopleWillRead.com), and holds forth on money and midlife at Surviving and Thriving (www.donnafreedman.com).

Donna lives in Anchorage, Alaska. On purpose.

Made in the USA
Middletown, DE
28 September 2016